BELGIUM 1

GUIDE 2023

The complete pocket tour guide to explore Brussel, Antwerp, Ghent, Flanders attractions with Belgian cuisines.

THOMAS HUMPHREY

Copyright © [2023] by [THOMAS HUMPHREY]

All rights reserved. No part of this publication may be reproduced, distributed, or transmitted in any form or by any means, including photocopying, recording, or other electronic or mechanical methods, without the prior written permission of the publisher, except in the case of brief quotations embodied in critical reviews and certain other noncommercial uses permitted by copyright law. For permission requests, please contact the publisher at the address below.

TABLE OF CONTENT

INTRODUCTION TO BELGIUM 7

About the country 11

Brussel city 15

History and culture 16

Geographical and climate features 19

Getting to Belgium and transportation 23

Visa Requirements 23

Getting to Belgium 26

Transportation Around Belgium: 28

CHAPTER 1 31

Welcome to Brussels 31

Overview and history of Brussels 33

.... 36

5 must see attraction in Brussel. 37

15 must try Food and drink in Brussel. 61

Shopping in Brussel 65

Accommodations in Brussel 69

.... 72

HOTEL VIEWS IN BRUSSELS 72

Events and festivals 73

CHAPTER 2 77

Welcome to Flanders regions 77

Overview and history 79

Welcome to Antwerp 82

5 Must see attraction in Antwerp. 84

4. Diamond district 97

Welcome to Ghent 104

5 must see attraction in Ghent 107

Welcome to Bruges 130

5 must see attractions in Bruges 135

Welcome to Leuven 155

5 must see attractions in Leuven. 159

Accommodations in Flanders 179

10 must try Food and drink in Flanders.......... 183

Events and festivals in Flanders...................... 188

CHAPTER 3 191

Welcome to Wallonia 191

Overview and history..................................... 193

Welcome to Namur... 198

5 must see attractions in Namur..................... 201

Welcome to Liège.. 220

5 must see attractions in Liege....................... 223

Welcome to Dinant... 240

5 must see attractions in Dinant..................... 243

Accommodations in Wallonia........................ 261

15 must try Food and drink in Wallonia......... 264

Events and festivals in Wallonia.................... 267

CHAPTER 5 OUTSIDE THE CITIES 271

Welcome to the Ardennes region.................... 271

5 must see attraction of ardenes region........... 274

Welcome to Coastal region............................. 289

5 must see attractions in the coastal region..... 291

Accommodations outside the city 304

Food and drink 307

Conclusion 310

INTRODUCTION TO BELGIUM

Welcome to The Western European nation of Belgium is a small but intriguing place. It is known for its rich history, stunning architecture, delicious cuisine, and famous exports such as chocolate, waffles, and beer. Belgium is also home to three distinct regions, each with its own unique culture and language: Flanders in the north, Wallonia in the south, and Brussels, the bilingual capital city.

The country has a long and storied past, with roots dating back to the Roman era. Over the centuries, Belgium has been shaped by various influences, including the rule of the Spanish, Austrian, and Dutch empires, as well as its own struggle for independence in the 19th century. Today, Belgium is a member of the European Union and has a thriving economy, making it a popular destination for tourists, business travelers, and expats alike.

Visitors to Belgium can enjoy a wide range of activities, from exploring the bustling streets of Brussels to hiking in the Ardennes Forest, visiting medieval castles and museums, or sampling some of the country's world-famous cuisine and beverages. With so much to offer, it's no wonder that Belgium is a favorite destination for travelers from all over the world.

Belgium is home to several iconic landmarks and attractions that draw visitors year-round. One of the most famous is the Grand Place in Brussels, a stunning central square surrounded by ornate guildhalls and the towering spires of the Brussels City Hall. Another must-see attraction is the Atomium, a massive steel structure shaped like a molecule that offers stunning views of the city from its observation deck.

Belgium is also known for its excellent cuisine, which ranges from hearty meat dishes to delicate pastries and chocolates. Belgian beer is also world-renowned, with hundreds of breweries producing everything from traditional abbey ales to fruity lambics and sour gauzes. Visitors can also indulge in the country's famous waffles, which are available in sweet and savory varieties, and the crispy fries that are typically served with mayonnaise.

Beyond its urban centers, Belgium is home to a wealth of natural beauty. The Ardennes region is known for its rolling hills, dense forests, and winding rivers, while the North Sea coast offers long stretches of sandy beaches and picturesque fishing villages. Visitors can also explore the country's network of canals and waterways, which offer scenic boat tours and opportunities for fishing and kayaking.

Whether you're a first-time visitor or a seasoned traveler, Belgium offers something for everyone. From its rich cultural heritage to its stunning natural landscapes and delicious cuisine, this small country has a big impact on anyone who visits. So why not start planning your own Belgian adventure today?

About the country

Belgium is a small country located in Western Europe, bordered by France, the Netherlands, Germany, and Luxembourg. It covers an area of approximately 30,500 square kilometers and has a population of around 11.6 million people.

The country has three official languages: Dutch, French, and German, with Dutch being the primary language in the Flemish region, French in Wallonia, and German in a small region in the east.

Belgium has a temperate maritime climate, with cool summers and mild winters. The country is known for its extensive road and rail network, making it easy to travel between cities and regions. The Euro is the official currency of Belgium, and it is part of the Schengen Area, which allows for free movement of people between participating countries.

Belgium is a constitutional monarchy, with a parliamentary system of government. The country has a long history, dating back to the Roman era, and has been shaped by various influences over the centuries, including the Spanish, Austrian, and Dutch empires. In 1830, Belgium declared independence from the Netherlands, becoming a sovereign nation.

Today, Belgium is a member of the European Union and has a thriving economy, with a strong focus on trade and services. The country is also known for its high quality of life, excellent healthcare system, and social welfare programs.

Belgium is home to several world-renowned institutions, including the European Union headquarters, NATO, and the World Customs Organization.

Belgium is a diverse and multicultural country, with a rich cultural heritage that includes art, music, and literature. It is also famous for its cuisine, which ranges from traditional Flemish stews and seafood dishes to French-inspired cuisine and chocolates. With its stunning architecture, natural beauty, and vibrant cities, Belgium is a popular destination for travelers from all over the world.

Belgium is a country with a rich cultural heritage and a long history of artistic achievement. The country has produced several world-renowned painters, such as Pieter Bruegel the Elder, Jan van Eyck, and René Magritte. Belgium is also known for its architecture, with stunning examples of Gothic, Renaissance, and Art Nouveau styles found throughout the country.

Belgium is divided into three regions: Flanders in the north, Wallonia in the south, and Brussels, which is a bilingual region and serves as the capital of both the country and the European Union. Each region has its own unique culture and traditions, with distinct languages, cuisine, and customs.

The country is also known for its beer culture, with over 1,500 varieties of beer produced by hundreds of breweries throughout the country. Belgian beer is renowned for its diversity, with styles ranging from Trappist ales to lambics and Saison's.

In terms of tourism, Belgium has a lot to offer. Visitors can explore the picturesque canals of Bruges, visit the historic city of Ghent, or discover the art and architecture of Brussels. The country is also home to several museums, including the Royal Museums of Fine Arts of Belgium, the Magritte Museum, and the Museum of Natural Sciences.

Belgium is a country that takes pride in its sustainability efforts, with a focus on green energy and environmentally friendly practices. The country has also made significant efforts to promote cycling and public transportation, making it easy for visitors to explore without relying on cars.

Overall, Belgium is a country that offers a unique blend of history, culture, and natural beauty. With its stunning architecture, delicious cuisine, and world-renowned beers, it is a destination that should be on every traveler's list.

Brussel city

History and culture

History

Belgium has a long and rich history, dating back to the Roman era. The country has been influenced by various empires over the centuries, including the Spanish, Austrian, and Dutch. In 1830, Belgium declared independence from the Netherlands and became a sovereign nation.

The country was invaded by Germany during World War I and World War II, resulting in significant damage and loss of life.

After World War II, Belgium emerged as a key player in the European Union, with Brussels serving as the headquarters for both the EU and NATO. Today, Belgium is known for its contributions to the fields of art, literature, and science, as well as its focus on sustainability and environmentally friendly practices.

Culture:

Belgium is a diverse and multicultural country, with a rich cultural heritage that includes art, music, and literature. The country has produced a number of world-renowned painters, such as Pieter Bruegel the Elder, Jan van Eyck, and René Magritte. Belgium is also known for its architecture, with stunning examples of Gothic, Renaissance, and Art Nouveau styles found throughout the country.

Belgium has several famous cultural festivals, including the Carnival of Binche, which is recognized by UNESCO as a Masterpiece of the Oral and Intangible Heritage of Humanity.

The festival involves elaborate costumes and masks, traditional dances, and music. Another popular festival is the Ghent Festival, which features music, theater, and street performances throughout the city.

Belgium is also famous for its cuisine, which includes a wide variety of dishes and flavors. Belgian cuisine is heavily influenced by French, Dutch, and

German cuisine, as well as local ingredients and traditions. Some popular dishes include moules-frites (mussels with fries), stomps (a potato and vegetable dish), and carbonade flamande (a hearty beef stew).

Beer is an important part of Belgian culture, with over 1,500 varieties of beer produced by hundreds of breweries throughout the country. Belgian beer is renowned for its diversity, with styles ranging from Trappist ales to lambics and Saison's.

In terms of music, Belgium has a vibrant music scene, with a focus on electronic and dance music. The country has produced a number of internationally renowned DJs, such as Dimitri Vegas & Like Mike, Lost Frequencies, and Charlotte de Witte.

Overall, Belgium is a country with a rich and diverse cultural heritage, offering a wide range of experiences for travelers interested in history, art, cuisine, and music.

Geographical and climate features

Belgium is a small country in Western Europe, bordered by the Netherlands to the north, Germany to the east, Luxembourg to the southeast, and France to the south and west. The country has a total area of 30,528 square kilometers and a population of approximately 11.7 million people.

Geographically, Belgium is a relatively flat country, with the highest point being Signal de Botrange, which stands at 694 meters (2,277 feet) above sea level. The country is also characterized by its many rivers and canals, including the Scheldt, Meuse, and Yser, which have played an important role in the country's history and economy.

Belgium has a temperate maritime climate, with mild winters and cool summers. The climate is influenced by the North Sea, which helps to moderate temperatures year-round. Average temperatures range from 0°C (32°F) in January to 18°C (64°F) in July. Rainfall is evenly distributed throughout the year, with an average of around 200 days of rain per year.

The country is divided into three regions: Flanders in the north, Wallonia in the south, and Brussels, which is a separate region and serves as the capital of both Belgium and the European Union. Each region has its own distinct geography and climate features, with Flanders being characterized by its flat landscapes and Wallonia by its hilly terrain.

Belgium has a diverse landscape that includes forests, farmland, and urban areas. The Ardennes Forest, located in the southeast part of the country, covers about a third of Wallonia and is known for its rugged hills and valleys. The forest is home to many species of wildlife, including wild boar, deer, and birds of prey.

In Flanders, the landscape is dominated by flat plains, except for the hilly Limburg region in the east. The region is known for its extensive network of canals, which are used for transportation and recreation. The Belgian coast, which stretches for 67 kilometers (42 miles) along the North Sea, is also a popular tourist destination.

Belgium's climate is influenced by the Gulf Stream, which brings warm water from the Gulf of Mexico to the North Atlantic Ocean. As a result, winters in Belgium are generally mild, with average temperatures ranging from 0°C (32°F) to 7°C (45°F). Summers are cooler than in many other parts of Europe, with average temperatures ranging from 18°C (64°F) to 23°C (73°F).

Rainfall is common throughout the year, with October and November being the wettest months. Snowfall is infrequent in most parts of the country, except for the Ardennes region, where snow is more common during the winter months.

Belgium is a highly urbanized country, with about 98% of the population living in urban areas. The largest cities in Belgium are Brussels, Antwerp, Ghent, and Charleroi. Brussels is the capital of both Belgium and the European Union and is home to many international organizations and diplomatic missions.

Oostende summer weather

Getting to Belgium and transportation

Belgium is a small country located in Western Europe, known for its medieval architecture, scenic canals, delicious chocolates, and famous beers. IIt is a well-known tourist destination that draws millions of travelers every year from all over the world. If you're planning a trip to Belgium, here is a guide on how to get there and get around the country.

Visa Requirements

Belgium is a part of the Schengen Area, a collection of 26 nations in Europe without external border controls. Therefore, if you are a citizen of a Schengen country, you do not need a visa to enter Belgium. Citizens of the European Union (EU), European Economic Area (EEA), and Switzerland can also enter Belgium without a visa. However, if you are a non-EU citizen, you may need a visa to enter Belgium, depending on your nationality.

Visa-Exempt Countries

Citizens of some countries can enter Belgium without a visa for a stay of up to 90 days in any 180-day period. These countries include:

Albania, Andorra, Antigua and Barbuda, Argentina, Australia, Bahamas, Barbados, Bosnia and Herzegovina, Brazil, Brunei Darussalam, Canada, Chile, Colombia, Costa Rica, Dominica, El Salvador, Georgia, Grenada, Guatemala, Honduras, Hong Kong (Special Administrative Region), Israel, Japan, Kiribati, Macao (Special Administrative Region), Macedonia, Malaysia, Marshall Islands, Mauritius, Mexico, Micronesia, Moldova, Monaco, Montenegro, New Zealand, Nicaragua, Palau, Panama, Paraguay, Peru, Saint Kitts and Nevis, Saint Lucia, Saint Vincent and the Grenadines, Samoa, San Marino, Serbia, Seychelles, Singapore, Solomon Islands, South Korea, Taiwan, Timor-Leste, Tonga, Trinidad and Tobago, Tuvalu, Ukraine, United Arab Emirates, United States of America, Uruguay, Vanuatu, Vatican City (Holy See)

Visa-Required Countries

Citizens of some countries need a visa to enter Belgium for any purpose, including tourism, business, or transit. These countries include: *Afghanistan, Algeria, Angola, Armenia, Azerbaijan, Bahrain, Bangladesh, Belarus, Belize, Benin, Bhutan, Bolivia, Botswana, Burkina Faso, Burundi, Cambodia, Cameroon, Cape Verde, Central African Republic, Chad, China, Comoros, Congo, Democratic Republic of the Congo, Cote d'Ivoire, Cuba, Djibouti, Dominican Republic, Ecuador, Egypt, Equatorial Guinea, Eritrea, Ethiopia, Fiji, Gabon, Gambia, Ghana, Guinea, Guinea-Bissau, Guyana, Haiti, India, Indonesia, Iran, Iraq, Jamaica, Jordan, Kazakhstan, Kenya, Kosovo, Kuwait, Kyrgyzstan, Laos, Lebanon, Lesotho, Liberia, Libya, Madagascar, Malawi, Maldives, Mali, Mauritania, Mongolia, Morocco ,Mozambique, Myanmar (Burma), Namibia, Nepal, Niger, Nigeria, North Korea, Oman ,Pakistan, Papua New Guinea*

Getting to Belgium

By Air:

Belgium has three main international airports, Brussels Airport, Antwerp Airport, and Charleroi Airport. Brussels Airport is the largest and busiest airport in Belgium, located in Zaventem, 12 km northeast of Brussels city center. It serves more than 260 destinations worldwide and is the primary hub for Belgium's national airline, Brussels Airlines. Antwerp Airport is a smaller airport that mainly serves regional flights to European destinations. Charleroi Airport is located 46 km south of Brussels and is the hub for low-cost airlines such as Ryanair and Wizz Air.

By Train:

Belgium has a well-developed railway network, and trains are a convenient way to travel within the country and from neighboring countries. Eurostar provides direct high-speed train services between London, Paris, and Brussels. Thalys trains operate from Paris, Amsterdam, and Cologne to Brussels, Antwerp, and other Belgian cities. The national railway company, SNCB, operates regional and intercity trains within Belgium, as well as international trains to neighboring countries such as the Netherlands, Germany, and France.

By Bus:

Bus travel is another affordable and convenient option for getting to Belgium from neighboring countries.

Flixbus and Euro lines are two of the major bus companies that operate services to Belgium from various European cities.

By Car:

Driving to Belgium is also possible, and the country is well-connected to neighboring countries via a network of highways. However, it is important to note that traffic can be heavy, especially during peak hours in major cities.

Transportation Around Belgium:

By Train:

As mentioned earlier, Belgium has an extensive railway network operated by the national railway company, SNCB. It is a convenient way to travel within the country and visit major cities such as Brussels, Antwerp, Ghent, and Bruges. Train tickets can be purchased at train stations or online, and discounts are available for students and seniors.

By Bus:

Local and regional bus services are also available in Belgium, operated by various companies such as De Lijn and STIB/MIVB. Bus services are affordable, and tickets can be purchased at bus stops or online. However, buses can be slower than trains, especially during peak hours.

By Tram:

Trams are available in major cities such as Brussels, Antwerp, and Ghent. They are a convenient and affordable way to travel within the city center and surrounding areas.

By Car:

Renting a car is another option for getting around Belgium, especially if you plan to explore rural areas and small towns. However, driving in major cities can be challenging due to heavy traffic and narrow roads.

In conclusion, Belgium is a beautiful country that can be easily reached by air, train, bus, or car. The country's well-developed transportation network makes it easy to get around and explore its many attractions. Whether you prefer to travel by train, bus, or car, there is a mode of transportation that will suit your needs and budget.

Antwerp train station

Brussel tram transportation

CHAPTER 1

Welcome to Brussels

Welcome to Brussels, the vibrant and multicultural capital city of Belgium. Situated in the heart of Europe, Brussels is a bustling metropolis that boasts a rich history, diverse culture, and world-renowned cuisine.

As the administrative center of the European Union, Brussels is home to an international community of diplomats, expats, and students, making it a truly global city. From its stunning architecture and historic landmarks to its lively nightlife and thriving art scene, Brussels has something to offer for everyone.

Whether you're a history buff, a foodie, or a lover of the arts, Brussels has plenty of attractions to keep you entertained. Discover the city's fascinating past by exploring its many museums and galleries, including the Royal Museums of Fine Arts of Belgium and the Belgian Comic Strip Center. Take a stroll through the iconic Grand Place, one of the most beautiful squares in the world, or marvel at the stunning Gothic architecture of the famous Brussels Cathedral.

For food lovers, Brussels is a paradise. From its famous waffles and chocolate to its world-renowned beer and moules-frites (mussels and fries), the city's culinary scene is second to none. Sample some of the local delicacies at one of the many restaurants and cafes scattered throughout the city, or visit the vibrant outdoor markets to sample the freshest local produce.

With its excellent public transport system and friendly locals, Brussels is an easy and enjoyable city to navigate. Whether you're here for a short stay or a longer visit, the city's unique charm and cultural diversity are sure to leave a lasting impression. So why not start planning your trip to Brussels today and discover all that this amazing city has to offer!

Overview and history of Brussels

Brussels is the capital city of Belgium, and it is also known as the administrative center of the European Union. This city is in the heart of Belgium, and it has a rich history, cultural diversity, and charming architecture that attract millions of tourists every year.

History:
Brussels was founded in the 10th century by a small community of fishermen and farmers. It quickly grew into an important trading center due to its strategic location between the regions of Flanders

and Wallonia. In the 15th century, Brussels became the capital of the Duchy of Brabant and played a significant role in European politics and commerce. During the 16th and 17th centuries, the city experienced a period of prosperity and cultural growth, which is evident in its stunning architecture.

In the 19th century, Brussels underwent significant urban development and expansion, and many of the city's iconic landmarks were built during this time, including the Grand Place, the Atomium, and the Royal Palace. During the two World Wars, Brussels played a crucial role in the resistance movement against German occupation.

In 1957, Brussels became the headquarters of the European Union, which has since transformed the city into an important international hub for politics, culture, and business.

Overview:

Today, Brussels is a vibrant city that offers a unique blend of modernity and tradition. It is renowned for its excellent cuisine, world-class museums, and stunning architecture. Visitors to Brussels can explore the charming, cobbled streets of the historic center, which is a UNESCO World Heritage Site, and marvel at the breathtaking Gothic and Baroque buildings that line the streets.

The city is home to many famous landmarks, including the Atomium, the Manneken Pis, the Royal Palace, and the impressive Grand Place. Visitors can also enjoy the city's excellent museums, such as the Magritte Museum, the Belgian Comic Strip Center, and the Museum of Modern Art.

Brussels is also famous for its cuisine, which includes dishes like moules frites, waffles, and chocolate. Visitors can indulge in these culinary delights in the many restaurants, cafes, and chocolatiers that dot the city.

In addition to its cultural and culinary attractions, Brussels is also an important center for business and commerce, with many multinational companies and organizations headquartered in the city.

Overall, Brussels is a fascinating city with a rich history and a vibrant culture. It is a must-visit destination for anyone traveling to Belgium, and it offers something for everyone, from history buffs and foodies to art lovers and business travelers.

Brussels map

5 must see attraction in Brussel.

1.Grand Place

The Grand Place, also known as Grote Markt in Dutch, is a historic square located in the heart of Brussels, the capital city of Belgium. It is one of the most iconic landmarks in Belgium, and a must-visit destination for anyone traveling to the country.

One of the most stunning squares in all of Europe, this same Grand Place has been a UNESCO World Heritage Site since 1998.

History of Grand Place

The Grand Place has a rich history dating back to the 11th century, when it was a simple market square. Over the centuries, the square has been transformed into the magnificent architectural masterpiece it is today.

The buildings surrounding the square are a blend of Gothic, Baroque, and neoclassical styles, reflecting the different periods of construction. The Grand Place has been the center of political and economic activity in Brussels for centuries, and it has been the site of many important events throughout Belgium's history.

Attractions and Activities

The Grand Place is home to many notable attractions that draw tourists from around the world. The most prominent building on the square is the Brussels Town Hall, a stunning Gothic structure that dates to the 15th century. The Town Hall is open to visitors, and you can take a guided tour to learn more about its history and see the beautiful interior.

Another highlight of the Grand Place is the Maison du Roi, or the King's House. This building was originally built as a bread market in the 16th century, but it was later converted into a museum that showcases the history of the city. The museum is home to many interesting exhibits, including costumes, tapestries, and paintings.

In addition to the historical buildings, the Grand Place is also known for its vibrant atmosphere. The square is surrounded by cafes, bars, and restaurants that offer a variety of Belgian specialties, such as waffles, chocolate, and beer. You can sit and enjoy a drink while taking in the stunning architecture and people-watching.

Events and Festivals

The Grand Place is also a popular venue for events and festivals throughout the year. One of the most famous events is the biennial flower carpet, which takes place every two years in August. The flower carpet is made up of more than 600,000 begonias arranged in a beautiful design that covers the entire square. It is a stunning sight to see and draws large crowds of visitors from all over the world.

Another popular event is the Brussels Christmas Market, which takes place during the holiday season. The market is filled with festive stalls selling gifts, food, and drinks, and there are often live music and other entertainment. The Grand Place is transformed into a winter wonderland, with a large Christmas tree and thousands of twinkling lights.

Getting There

The Grand Place is in the center of Brussels, and it is easily accessible by public transportation. The closest metro station is Bourse/Beurs, which is served by lines 3 and 4. The square is also within walking distance of many other popular attractions in the city, such as the Manneken Pis statue and the Royal Palace of Brussels.

The Grand Place is a must-visit destination for anyone traveling to Belgium. Its stunning architecture, rich history, and vibrant atmosphere make it one of the most beautiful squares in Europe.

Whether you are interested in history, culture, or food, the Grand Place has something to offer everyone. So, if you're planning a trip to Belgium, be sure to include a visit to this iconic landmark on your itinerary.

2. Manneken Pis

Manneken Pis is a famous bronze statue in Brussels, Belgium, that depicts a little boy urinating into a fountain basin. It is one of the most popular tourist attractions in the city and is a symbol of Belgium's unique sense of humor and irreverence. Here is a comprehensive guide to Manneken Pis, including its history, location, and interesting facts.

History

The exact origin of Manneken Pis is unknown, but it is believed to have been created in the early 17th century. The statue was originally made out of stone, but it was later replaced with a bronze replica in 1619. Over the years, the statue has been stolen, damaged, and replaced several times. The current version of Manneken Pis was installed in 1965 and is a replica of the original bronze statue.

Location

Manneken Pis is located in the heart of Brussels, just a short walk from the Grand Place. The statue is situated at the junction of Rue de l'Etuve and Rue du Chêne, near the Brussels City Museum. It is easy to spot the statue due to its small size and central location. Many visitors to Brussels make a point to see the statue and take a photo with it.

Interesting Facts

Manneken Pis has become a symbol of Brussels and is a popular tourist attraction. The following are some fascinating statuary-related details:

There are many legends and stories about the origins of Manneken Pis, including one that tells of a young boy who saved the city by urinating on a burning fuse.

The statue is dressed in various outfits throughout the year, which are provided by different organizations and countries. There are over 1,000 outfits in the statue's wardrobe.

Manneken Pis is not the only urinating statue in Brussels. There are two others: Jeanneke Pis, a female version of the statue, and Zinneke Pis, a dog version.

The statue has been stolen several times throughout its history, including once by French soldiers in 1747.

The statue is connected to a complex system of pipes and drains that allows it to "urinate" on special occasions, such as national holidays.

In 2014, a chocolate version of Manneken Pis was created to celebrate the statue's 400th anniversary.

The statue has become so famous that there are replicas of it in other countries, including Japan and the United States.

Visiting Manneken Pis

If you are visiting Brussels, a visit to Manneken Pis is a must. The statue is easily accessible and free to view. You can take photos with the statue and admire its unique design. If you are lucky, you may even see the statue dressed in one of its many outfits. Manneken Pis is a fun and quirky symbol of Belgium's irreverent sense of humor, and a great addition to any travel itinerary.

Getting there

Getting to Manneken Pis is easy, as it is in the heart of Brussels and is easily accessible by public transportation or on foot.

By public transportation:

Metro: The nearest metro station is Bourse/Beurs, which is located just a few minutes' walk from the statue.

Bus: Several bus lines stop near Manneken Pis, including the 48, 95, and 96.

On foot:

Walking is the most convenient way to get to Manneken Pis if you are staying in the city center. The statue is located just a short walk from the Grand Place and other popular tourist attractions.

By bike:

Brussels has a public bike-sharing system called Villo! and there are several bike stations located near Manneken Pis.

By car:

Driving in Brussels can be challenging due to heavy traffic and limited parking. If you do choose to drive, there are several paid parking lots located near Manneken Pis.

It is important to note that the area around Manneken Pis can be quite crowded, especially during peak tourist season. It is best to visit early in the morning or later in the evening to avoid the crowds.

3. Atomium

Atomium is a stunning building located in Brussels, Belgium. It is one of the most iconic landmarks of the city and is a must-visit attraction for anyone traveling to Belgium. Built in 1958 for the World Expo, Atomium has become a symbol of modern architecture and scientific progress.

The Atomium was designed by engineer Andre Waterkeyn and architects Andre and Jean Polak. The building was inspired by the structure of an iron atom, with the nine spheres representing the nine electrons of the atom. The Atomium stands at 102 meters high and weighs around 2,400 tons.

The Atomium is open to visitors year-round and offers stunning views of Brussels from the top. Visitors can take the elevator to the top sphere and enjoy panoramic views of the city. Inside the building, visitors can explore the different spheres, which house various exhibitions and displays.

One of the most popular exhibitions in the Atomium is the permanent exhibition on the history of the building and the World Expo.

Visitors can learn about the building's construction, its significance in Belgian history, and the various events that have taken place at the Atomium over the years.

Another popular exhibition is the temporary exhibition, which changes regularly and focuses on different themes related to science, technology, and innovation.

These exhibitions are always engaging and interactive, with plenty of hands-on activities and displays to keep visitors entertained.

The Atomium also has a restaurant located in the top sphere, which offers stunning views of the city and serves a range of Belgian and international dishes. Additionally, there is a gift shop where guests can buy keepsakes and souvenirs.

In addition to the Atomium itself, visitors can also explore the surrounding area, which includes the Mini-Europe Park and the Brussels Planetarium. Mini-Europe is a miniature park that features replicas of famous European landmarks, while the Brussels Planetarium offers educational shows and exhibits about space and astronomy.

The Atomium is a must-visit attraction for anyone traveling to Belgium. It offers a unique and fascinating glimpse into the history of the country and the World Expo, as well as providing stunning views of Brussels from the top. Whether you're interested in science, architecture, or just want to see one of the most iconic landmarks in Belgium, the Atomium is worth a visit.

Getting there

Getting to the Atomium is relatively easy, as it is in the north of Brussels and is well-connected to the city's public transportation system.

By Metro: The easiest way to reach the Atomium is by metro. You can take Line 6 to the Heysel/Heizel station, which is located just a short walk from the Atomium. The metro runs regularly and is a fast and convenient way to get to the Atomium.

By Bus: There are several bus routes that stop near the Atomium, including bus lines 84, 88, and 89. These buses connect the Atomium to various parts of the city, and you can plan your journey using the STIB/MIVB website or app.

By Car: If you're driving to the Atomium, there is a large parking lot nearby where you can park your car for a fee. However, it is worth noting that parking in

Brussels can be difficult and expensive, so taking public transportation may be a better option.

By Bicycle: The Atomium is also accessible by bike, and there are several bike lanes that lead to the attraction. You can rent a bike from one of the city's many bikes rental companies or use a shared bike scheme such as Villo.

No matter which mode of transportation you choose, it is important to plan your journey in advance and leave plenty of time to get to the Atomium, especially during peak tourist season.

4. Royal Palace of Brussels

The Royal Palace of Brussels is one of the most iconic landmarks of Belgium and is a must-visit attraction for any traveler visiting the country. The palace serves as the official residence of the Belgian royal family and is in the heart of Brussels, the capital city of Belgium.

History of the Royal Palace:

The Royal Palace of Brussels was first built in the 18th century when the city of Brussels was still part of the Austrian Netherlands. The palace was initially constructed as a modest mansion for the Prince of

Orange, who was the governor of the city at that time. However, over the years, the palace underwent several renovations and expansions to become the magnificent structure that it is today.

During the 19th and early 20th centuries, the palace was home to several monarchs of Belgium, including King Leopold II and King Albert I. The palace was also the site of many important historical events, such as the signing of the Treaty of Brussels in 1948, which led to the formation of NATO.

The Royal Palace Today:

Today, the Royal Palace of Brussels serves primarily as a venue for state events and official receptions. The palace is open to the public during the summer months, from July to September, when visitors can explore the grandiose interior of the palace and its stunning gardens.

The interior of the palace features an impressive collection of artwork, furniture, and decor that reflect the rich history and culture of Belgium. Visitors can admire the ornate throne room, the lavish ballroom, and the elegant drawing rooms. The palace also houses a collection of tapestries that were created by Flemish artisans in the 16th century.

The palace's gardens are equally impressive, with several beautifully manicured lawns, fountains, and flower beds. The gardens are a popular spot for picnics and relaxation, and visitors can take a leisurely stroll through the grounds while admiring the stunning architecture of the palace.

Visiting the Royal Palace:

The Royal Palace of Brussels is open to the public during the summer months, from July to September. Admission to the palace is free, and visitors are encouraged to take a guided tour to fully appreciate the palace's history and significance.

Visitors should note that the palace may be closed during official state events or if the royal family is in residence. It is advisable to check the palace's website before planning a visit to ensure that it is open to the public.

In conclusion, the Royal Palace of Brussels is a must-visit attraction for anyone traveling to Belgium. The palace is a symbol of Belgium's rich history and culture and offers visitors a glimpse into the lives of its monarchs. Whether you're interested in art, architecture, or history, the Royal Palace of Brussels is a must-see destination that should not be missed.

Getting there

The Royal Palace of Brussels is located in the heart of Brussels, the capital city of Belgium, and can be easily accessed by public transportation or by car.

By Public Transportation:

The palace is well-connected to the city's public transportation network, with several bus and tram stops located nearby. The closest metro station is Parc/Park, which is just a short walk away.

By Car:

If you're driving to the palace, there are several parking garages located nearby where you can park your car. However, be aware that parking in the city center can be quite expensive, so it may be more cost-effective to use public transportation instead.

Alternatively, you can also take a taxi or an Uber to the palace, which is a convenient option if you're traveling with a group or have a lot of luggage.

No matter how you choose to get there, be sure to allow plenty of time to explore the palace and its surroundings, as there's plenty to see and do in this beautiful part of Brussels.

5. Belgian Comic Strip Center

The Belgian Comic Strip Center, also known as the Centre Belge de la Bande Dessinée (CBBD), is a museum and cultural institution located in Brussels, Belgium. It is dedicated to the art of comic books and is considered one of the most important centers of its kind in the world.

History:

The Belgian Comic Strip Center was founded in 1989 and is housed in a building designed by Victor Horta, one of the most important architects of the Art Nouveau movement. The building, which was originally a department store, was renovated specifically for the purpose of housing the museum.

Exhibitions:

The museum's permanent exhibition covers the history of Belgian comic books, from their origins in the 1920s to the present day. The exhibition includes original artwork, sketches, and manuscripts from some of the most famous Belgian comic book authors, such as Hergé, the creator of Tintin, and Peyo, the creator of The Smurfs. Visitors can also see how comic books are made and learn about the different techniques used by artists.

In addition to the permanent exhibition, the museum also hosts temporary exhibitions that showcase different aspects of the comic book industry. Recent exhibitions have focused on female comic book artists, the impact of Belgian comic books on international culture, and the use of comic books in education.

Activities:

The Belgian Comic Strip Center also offers a variety of activities for visitors of all ages. One of the most popular activities is the comic book workshop, where visitors can learn how to create their own comic book pages under the guidance of a professional artist. The museum also hosts guided tours, film screenings, and lectures on comic book art and history.

Shop and Restaurant:

The museum also has a shop where visitors can purchase comic books, graphic novels, and other merchandise related to the world of comic books. The shop has a wide selection of books in several languages, including English, French, and Dutch.

The Belgian Comic Strip Center also has a restaurant, which serves traditional Belgian cuisine and offers a panoramic view of the city. The restaurant is located on the top floor of the museum and is a great place to relax and enjoy the view after exploring the exhibitions.

Visiting:

The Belgian Comic Strip Center is open every day except for Mondays, and admission is €10 for adults, €7 for seniors and students, and free for children under 12. The museum is in the heart of Brussels, just a few minutes' walk from the Grand Place and other major tourist attractions.

Conclusion:

The Belgian Comic Strip Center is a must-see destination for anyone interested in the world of comic books. With its extensive collection of original artwork, informative exhibitions, and fun activities, it offers a unique and entertaining experience for visitors of all ages. So, don't miss the opportunity to visit this amazing museum while in Brussels.

15 must try Food and drink in Brussel.

Brussels, the capital of Belgium, is a vibrant and multicultural city with a rich culinary heritage. From traditional Belgian dishes to international cuisine, Brussels offers a diverse range of food and drink options. Here are 15 must-try foods and drinks in Brussels that will satisfy your taste buds:

Belgian Waffles: One of the most iconic Belgian dishes, Belgian waffles are crispy on the outside and soft on the inside. They are often topped with whipped cream, fresh fruit, and chocolate sauce.

Moules-frites: This classic Belgian dish consists of mussels cooked in white wine and served with fries. It is typically served with mayonnaise or aioli.

Chocolate: Belgium is famous for its chocolate, and Brussels is home to some of the best chocolatiers in the world. You can find everything from truffles to pralines, and even chocolate sculptures.

Frites: Belgium is also famous for its fries, which are served in a paper cone with a variety of sauces such as mayonnaise, ketchup, and curry ketchup.

Stoemp: A traditional Belgian dish, stoemp is a mashed potato dish mixed with vegetables such as carrots, onions, and leeks.

Beer: Belgium is known for its beer, and Brussels is home to numerous breweries and beer bars. Some popular Belgian beers include Duvel, Chimay, and Hoegaarden.

Speculoos: These spiced short crust biscuits are a popular treat in Belgium and are often served with coffee or tea.

Carbonade Flamande: This hearty beef stew is made with beer and served with crusty bread or French fries.

Waterzooi: A creamy fish or chicken soup, Waterzooi is a staple of Belgian cuisine.

Pistolets: These small crusty rolls are often filled with cheese, ham, or a variety of other ingredients.

Jenever: A traditional Belgian liquor, Jenever is a type of gin that is typically served with a side of pickles or cheese.

Tarte au Sucre: This sweet pastry is made with sugar, butter, and cream, and is a popular dessert in Belgium.

Croquettes: These small fried balls are often filled with cheese, meat, or vegetables and are a popular snack in Brussels.

Peperkoek: A spiced gingerbread cake, Peperkoek is often served with coffee or tea.

Gueuze: This sour beer is a specialty of Brussels and is made by blending young and old lambic beers.

Shopping in Brussel

Shopping in Brussels is a delightful experience that is sure to appeal to all tastes and budgets. From designer boutiques to quaint specialty shops, the Belgian capital offers a wide range of shopping opportunities for visitors. Whether you're looking for high-end fashion, handcrafted souvenirs, or delicious Belgian chocolates, Brussels has it all.

Shopping Districts

The city of Brussels has several shopping districts, each with its own unique character and style. The most popular districts include:

Rue Neuve: This pedestrianized shopping street is the busiest shopping district in Brussels, with over 200 shops and department stores. It is the perfect place to find high-street fashion and accessories, as well as electronics and home goods.

Sablon: The Sablon district is known for its high-end fashion boutiques, antique shops, and art galleries. The area has a charming old-world atmosphere and is a great place to find luxury goods and unique souvenirs.

Avenue Louise: This prestigious shopping district is home to some of the most exclusive fashion boutiques and designer stores in Brussels. It is also the place to find luxury spas, gourmet food shops, and high-end home decor.

Marolles: The Marolles district is known for its antique shops and flea markets. Here, you can find vintage furniture, unique collectibles, and rare books.

Shopping Centers

Brussels also has several modern shopping centers, which are popular with locals and tourists alike. The most popular shopping centers include:

City 2: Located on Rue Neuve, City 2 is the largest shopping center in Brussels. It has over 100 stores and is home to popular brands like H&M, Zara, and Primark.

Galeries Royales Saint-Hubert: This historic shopping arcade is one of the oldest shopping centers in Europe, dating back to 1847. It is a beautiful place to shop, with its glass ceiling, ornate decorations, and high-end boutiques.

Woluwe Shopping Center: Located in the eastern suburbs of Brussels, Woluwe Shopping Center is one of the largest shopping centers in Belgium. It has over 130 stores, including popular brands like Apple, Adidas, and Levi's.

Souvenirs and Gifts

Belgium is known for its high-quality chocolates, beers, and lace, making these popular souvenirs for tourists. The best places to find these gifts include:

Chocolaterie Mary: This historic chocolate shop has been in business since 1919 and is known for its artisanal chocolates and pralines.

Maison Dandoy: This bakery is known for its traditional Belgian cookies, including speculoos and gingerbread.

Brussels Beer Project: This craft brewery is known for its innovative beers, including a chocolate stout and a Belgian IPA.

Sablon Lace: This lace shop has been in business since 1952 and is known for its high-quality lace products, including tablecloths, napkins, and doilies.

Conclusion

Shopping in Brussels is a fun and diverse experience that caters to all tastes and budgets. Whether you're looking for high-end fashion or unique souvenirs, Brussels has something to offer. With its numerous shopping districts, modern shopping centers, and specialty shops, Brussels is a shopper's paradise that should not be missed on any trip to Belgium.

Accommodations in Brussel

When planning a trip to Brussels, one of the most important aspects to consider is where to stay. Fortunately, Brussels offers a wide range of accommodation options to suit every traveler's preference and budget. Whether you're looking for a luxurious hotel, a cozy bed and breakfast, or a budget-friendly hostel, Brussels has something to offer.

In this guide, we'll explore some of the top accommodation options in Brussels.

Hotels Brussels is home to many hotels, ranging from luxury hotels to more affordable options. Some of the most popular luxury hotels in Brussels include the Hotel Amigo, the Sofitel Brussels Le Louise, and the Steigenberger Witcher's. These hotels offer top-notch amenities such as fine dining restaurants, fitness centers, and spas, as well as stylish and spacious rooms.

For those looking for more affordable hotel options, there are several chain hotels located throughout Brussels, including the Novotel, Ibis, and Mercure hotels. These hotels offer comfortable rooms at a more reasonable price point, often with amenities such as free Wi-Fi and breakfast included.

Bed and Breakfasts For a more intimate and homier feel, consider staying at a bed and breakfast in Brussels. There are many charming bed and breakfasts located throughout the city, offering cozy rooms and personalized service. Some popular options include the B&B L'Art de la Fugue, the B&B Les Cousins de Bruxelles, and the B&B Le Valduc.

Hostels For budget-conscious travelers, hostels are a great option for accommodation in Brussels. There are several hostels located throughout the city, offering affordable dormitory-style rooms as well as private rooms. Some popular hostels in Brussels include the Meininger Brussels City Center, the

Brussels 2GO4 Quality Hostel, and the Generation Europe Youth Hostel.

Airbnb Another option for accommodation in Brussels is to rent an apartment or room through Airbnb. There are many listings available throughout the city, offering a range of options from budget-friendly shared rooms to luxurious private apartments. Staying in an Airbnb can also provide a more authentic and local experience, allowing you to live like a local during your stay in Brussels.

Location When choosing where to stay in Brussels, it's important to consider location. The city is divided into several neighborhoods, each with its own character and attractions. Some popular neighborhoods to consider include the city center, which is home to many of the city's famous landmarks and attractions, as well as the trendy neighborhoods of Ixelles and Saint-Gilles.

Conclusion No matter what your budget or preferences, Brussels offers a wide range of accommodation options to suit every traveler's needs. From luxury hotels to cozy bed and breakfasts, there's something for everyone in this vibrant and historic city. When planning your trip to Brussels, be sure to consider your accommodation options carefully to ensure a comfortable and enjoyable stay.

HOTEL VIEWS IN BRUSSELS

Events and festivals

Brussels, the capital city of Belgium, is a melting pot of cultures and home to some of the most popular events and festivals in the country. From beer festivals to music concerts, Brussels has something to offer for everyone. Here are some of the top events and festivals to check out in Brussels:

Brussels Christmas Market the Brussels Christmas Market is one of the most popular events in the city, attracting thousands of visitors every year. The market features over 240 stalls selling everything from handmade crafts to traditional Belgian treats like waffles and chocolate. There are also plenty of festive activities to enjoy, including ice-skating, a Ferris wheel, and live music performances.

Belgian Beer Weekend Belgium is famous for its beer, and the Belgian Beer Weekend is the perfect opportunity to sample some of the country's best brews. The festival takes place in September and features over 400 different beers from more than 50

Belgian breweries. Visitors can also enjoy food stalls and live music throughout the event.

Brussels Jazz Marathon the Brussels Jazz Marathon is a three-day event that takes place every May and features over 100 free jazz concerts throughout the city. The festival showcases a range of jazz styles, from traditional to contemporary, and takes place in a variety of venues, including bars, clubs, and concert halls.

Belgian Pride Belgian Pride is a celebration of LGBTQ+ culture and rights and takes place every May in Brussels. The festival features a parade through the city center, with colorful floats, costumes, and music. There are also plenty of parties, concerts, and cultural events taking place throughout the week.

Fête de l'Iris Fête de l'Iris is a celebration of the Brussels region and takes place every May. The festival features live music, street performances, food stalls, and a parade showcasing the region's cultural heritage. There are also plenty of family-friendly activities, including a children's village and a fairground.

Brussels Food Truck Festival the Brussels Food Truck Festival is a four-day event that takes place every May and features over 100 food trucks serving a variety of international cuisine. The festival takes place in the city's Bois de la Cambre Park and also features live music, games, and activities for all ages.

Brussels Flower Carpet the Brussels Flower Carpet is a biennial event that takes place in August and transforms the Grand Place square into a stunning floral display. The carpet is made up of over 500,000 begonias, arranged into intricate patterns and designs. Visitors can admire the carpet from above on the balcony of the Brussels City Hall or from ground level in the square itself.

Couleur Café Festival the Couleur Café Festival is a three-day event that takes place every June and celebrates the diversity of world music. The festival features live music performances from a range of genres, including reggae, hip-hop, and electronic music. There are also food stalls, art exhibitions, and cultural activities taking place throughout the event.

In conclusion, Brussels is a city with a vibrant cultural scene and plenty of events and festivals throughout the year. Whether you're interested in music, food, or cultural celebrations, there's something for everyone in the Belgian capital.

CHAPTER 2

Welcome to Flanders regions.

Welcome to Flanders, a region in the northern part of Belgium known for its rich history, vibrant cities, picturesque countryside, and delicious cuisine. Flanders offers visitors a unique blend of old-world charm and modern-day energy, making it a must-visit destination for travelers from around the world.

Whether you're exploring the medieval streets of Bruges, wandering through the art-filled galleries of Antwerp, or savoring the culinary delights of Ghent, Flanders has something to offer everyone. The region is home to countless museums, galleries, and historical landmarks, including the famous Cathedral of Our Lady in Antwerp, the Gothic town hall in Leuven, and the stunning Castle of the Counts in Ghent.

In addition to its urban centers, Flanders is also famous for its picturesque countryside, which features rolling hills, lush forests, and quaint villages. Visitors can explore the region's natural beauty by taking a leisurely bike ride along one of the many cycling routes or hiking through the Ardennes Forest.

No trip to Flanders is complete without indulging in the region's renowned cuisine, which features a mix of French and Dutch influences. From savory dishes like moules-frites (mussels and fries) and stoofvlees (beef stew) to sweet treats like Belgian waffles and chocolate, Flanders is a food lover's paradise.

So, whether you're a history buff, a nature lover, or a foodie, Flanders is the perfect destination for your next adventure. Come discover the beauty and charm of this enchanting region and create memories that will last a lifetime.

Overview and history

Flanders is a region in Belgium that is in the northern part of the country. It has a distinguished history, beautiful architecture, and a thriving culture. This region has a long and complex history, which is reflected in its diverse cultural traditions and distinct identity.

Overview of Flanders:

Flanders is one of the three regions of Belgium, along with Wallonia and Brussels. It is made up of five provinces: West Flanders, East Flanders, Antwerp, Flemish Brabant, and Limburg. The region covers an area of approximately 13,500 square kilometers and has a population of around 6.6 million people.

Flanders is known for its beautiful cities, such as Brussels, Bruges, Ghent, and Antwerp. These cities are home to many historic landmarks, such as the Grand Place in Brussels, the Belfry of Bruges, and the Cathedral of Our Lady in Antwerp.

Flanders is also known for its excellent food, beer, and chocolate. The region is home to many famous breweries, such as Stella Artois and Duvel, and produces some of the world's best chocolate.

History of Flanders:

The history of Flanders dates to the Middle Ages when it was an important center of trade and commerce. During this time, the region was ruled by a powerful class of nobles who were known as the Counts of Flanders. They built many impressive castles and cathedrals, which can still be seen today. In the 14th and 15th centuries, Flanders became an important center of the Renaissance. The region was home to many famous artists, such as Jan van Eyck, Rogier van der Weyden, and Hans Memling. They created many beautiful works of art that can still be seen in museums and galleries throughout the region. During the 16th century, Flanders was ruled by the Habsburgs, who were based in Austria. They brought many changes to the region, including the introduction of the Protestant Reformation. This led to a period of religious conflict, which lasted for many years.

In the 19th century, Flanders became an important center of industry, with many factories and mills being built in the region. This led to a period of economic growth and prosperity, which continued into the 20th century.

Today, Flanders is a vibrant and modern region that is known for its rich cultural heritage and excellent quality of life. It is home to many universities and research institutions, which are helping to drive innovation and progress in a wide range of fields.

In conclusion, Flanders is a region of Belgium that is rich in history, culture, and tradition. Whether you are interested in art, architecture, food, or beer, there is something for everyone in this beautiful and fascinating region.

Welcome to Antwerp

Antwerp is a captivating city located in the northern part of Belgium, known for its rich history, stunning architecture, and vibrant culture. As the second largest city in Belgium, Antwerp is a hub of creativity, fashion, and design, making it a must-visit destination for travelers from all over the world.

As a major port city, Antwerp has a long and fascinating history that dates to the Middle Ages. It played a crucial role in the development of the European economy and was once one of the wealthiest cities in the world. Today, visitors can still see the remnants of this prosperous past in the city's stunning buildings, museums, and galleries.

Antwerp is also renowned for its fashion and design scene, which has produced some of the most innovative and avant-garde designers in the world. The city is home to the Royal Academy of Fine Arts, which has nurtured some of the most talented artists and designers in the world, including the legendary fashion designer, Dries Van Noten.

Beyond the cultural offerings, Antwerp is also a food lover's paradise, with a wide variety of restaurants, cafes, and bars serving up some of the most delicious cuisine in Belgium. Whether you're in the mood for traditional Flemish dishes like stoverij and frietjes or international fare like sushi and pizza, Antwerp has something for everyone.

Overall, Antwerp is a dynamic and exciting city that should be on every traveler's itinerary when visiting Belgium. With its rich history, stunning architecture, vibrant culture, and world-class cuisine, it is a destination that is sure to captivate and inspire visitors of all ages and interests.

5 Must see attraction in Antwerp.

1. Cathedral of Our Lady

The Cathedral of Our Lady, also known as Onze-Lieve-Vrouwekathedraal in Dutch, is a breathtaking Gothic cathedral located in the heart of Antwerp, Belgium. It is one of the most impressive landmarks of the city and a must-see for anyone visiting Belgium. The cathedral is dedicated to the Virgin Mary and is the largest Gothic church in the Low Countries.

History

Construction of the Cathedral of Our Lady began in 1352, but the building was not completed until the 16th century. Over the centuries, the cathedral has undergone numerous renovations and restorations. During World War II, the cathedral was severely damaged by bombs, but it was rebuilt and restored to its former glory in the years that followed.

Architecture

The Cathedral of Our Lady is a masterpiece of Gothic architecture. The cathedral's soaring spire is 123 meters (404 feet) tall, making it the tallest church tower in Belgium. The interior of the cathedral is just as impressive, with stunning stained-glass windows, intricate stone carvings, and a magnificent altarpiece by the famous artist Rubens. The cathedral also houses numerous works of art and religious artifacts.

Things to see and do.

One of the main attractions of the Cathedral of Our Lady is the altarpiece by Rubens. The triptych, which depicts the Assumption of the Virgin Mary, is considered one of the artist's greatest works. Visitors can also climb the cathedral's tower for a panoramic view of Antwerp and the surrounding area. The climb is challenging, but the view from the top is well worth the effort.

Another highlight of the cathedral is the treasury, which houses a collection of religious artifacts and artworks, including silverware, tapestries, and paintings. Visitors can also explore the crypt, which contains the remains of many important figures from Antwerp's history.

Visiting information

The Cathedral of Our Lady is open to visitors daily from 10:00 am to 5:00 pm. Admission is free, but there is a fee to climb the tower or visit the treasury. Guided tours of the cathedral are also available for a fee. Visitors should dress appropriately when visiting the cathedral, covering their shoulders and knees out of respect for the religious nature of the building.

Getting there

The Cathedral of Our Lady is in the heart of Antwerp, Belgium, and is easily accessible by various modes of transportation.

By train: Antwerp has a central train station, Antwerpen-Centraal, which is located about a 10–15-minute walk from the cathedral. From the train station, visitors can take the following routes to reach the cathedral: Tram 3, 5, 9 or 15 to Groenplaats, or Tram 2, 6, 7 or 15 to Meir.

By bus: Visitors can take bus lines 22 or 180 to reach the cathedral.

By car: Visitors can park at one of the many parking garages located near the cathedral, such as Parking Grote Markt, Parking Meir, or Parking Groenplaats.

By bike: Antwerp has a bike-sharing system, Velo Antwerpen, which has bike stations located throughout the city. Visitors can rent a bike and ride to the cathedral.

By foot: The Cathedral of Our Lady is located in the historic city center of Antwerp, and is easily accessible by foot. Visitors can explore the city on foot and enjoy the sights along the way.

Conclusion

The Cathedral of Our Lady is a magnificent example of Gothic architecture and a must-see for anyone visiting Antwerp or Belgium. Whether you are interested in art, history, or religion, there is something for everyone at this impressive cathedral. With its towering spire, stunning stained-glass windows, and impressive altarpiece by Rubens, the Cathedral of Our Lady is truly a sight to behold.

2. Rubens House

The Rubens House, located in Antwerp, Belgium, is one of the city's most important cultural landmarks. The museum is dedicated to the life and work of the famous Baroque painter Peter Paul Rubens, who lived in the house from 1610 to 1640. The Rubens House is home to an extensive collection of Rubens' works, as well as works by his contemporaries and predecessors.

Getting to the Rubens House is relatively easy, as Antwerp is well-connected to other major cities in

Belgium and the rest of Europe. Here's everything you need to know about visiting the Rubens House and getting there.

Getting to the Rubens House

By Train: Antwerp is easily accessible by train from Brussels, Ghent, Bruges, and other major cities in Belgium. From Antwerp Central Station, you can take tram 2 or 15 to the Rubens House. The nearest tram stop is "Rubenshuis".

By Car: If you're driving, there are several parking options available in Antwerp. The nearest car park to the Rubens House is "Q-Park Rubens", which is located on Rubenslei 15, just a short walk from the museum.

By Bike: Antwerp is a very bike-friendly city, and there are bike racks available near the Rubens House. You can also rent a bike from one of the many bike rental companies in the city.

Visiting the Rubens House

The Rubens House is open Tuesday through Sunday from 10 am to 5 pm, with extended hours on Wednesday until 8 pm. The museum is closed on

Mondays, as well as on January 1st, May 1st, November 1st, and December 25th.

Admission to the Rubens House is €12 for adults, €10 for seniors, and €2 for visitors under the age of 26. Visitors under the age of 12 are admitted free of charge. Guided tours of the museum are also available for an additional fee.

Inside the Rubens House, you'll find an impressive collection of paintings, sculptures, and other works of art. The museum is organized into several rooms, each with its own unique theme. Some of the highlights of the collection include Rubens' "Descent from the Cross", "The Four Philosophers", and "The Miracles of St. Ignatius". You'll also find works by other Flemish artists, such as Anthony van Dyck and Jacob Jordaens.

In addition to the artwork, the Rubens House also offers a glimpse into the life of Peter Paul Rubens. You can explore the artist's former living quarters, including his studio and bedroom, which have been restored to their original condition. The museum also features a beautiful garden, which is the perfect place to relax and enjoy the scenery after your visit.

Conclusion

The Rubens House is a must-visit destination for art lovers and history buffs alike. With its impressive collection of artwork, fascinating history, and beautiful gardens, the museum offers something for everyone. And with its central location in Antwerp and easy accessibility by train, car, or bike, it's easy to plan a visit to the Rubens House as part of your Belgium travel itinerary.

3. Central Station

Central Station, also known as Brussels Central Station, is one of the main transportation hubs in the city of Brussels, Belgium. It is in the heart of the city, close to many tourist attractions, making it a popular destination for travelers. In this guide, we'll provide comprehensive information about the Central Station and how to get there.

About Central Station

Central Station is a beautiful and historic train station that was built in the late 19th century. It is a stunning example of the architectural style of that period, featuring a massive dome and grand façade. The station is not only an important transportation hub but also a tourist attraction.

Central Station serves both domestic and international trains, making it a crucial link between Brussels and other major European cities. The station has many amenities, including food stalls, cafes, shops, and luggage storage facilities. It also has a tourist office, where visitors can get maps, brochures, and other travel information.

Getting to Central Station

There are several ways to get to Central Station, including by train, bus, metro, and taxi. Below we provide detailed information on each of these options.

By Train

If you are traveling to Brussels from another city in Belgium, you can take a train to Central Station. The station is served by several train companies, including Belgian Railways (SNCB/NMBS), Eurostar, and Thalys. Trains run regularly to and from cities like Antwerp, Ghent, Bruges, and Liege, as well as Paris, London, and Amsterdam.

By Bus

Several bus companies operate in Brussels, and many of them stop at or near Central Station. Eurolines, Flixbus, and Megabus are just a few examples of companies that serve Brussels. The bus terminal is close to the train station.

By Metro

The metro is an excellent way to get around Brussels, and Central Station is served by several metro lines. The station is located on lines 1 and 5, which run through the city center and connect to other metro lines. You can take the metro to and from many parts of the city, including the airport.

By Taxi

Taxis are widely available in Brussels, and you can easily hail one from any part of the city. Taxis are a convenient way to get to Central Station, especially if you have a lot of luggage. However, they can be expensive, so be sure to check the fare before getting in.

Conclusion

Central Station is a vital transportation hub in Brussels, and getting there is relatively easy. Whether you are traveling by train, bus, metro, or taxi, you can reach the station quickly and conveniently. Once you arrive, you can take advantage of the many amenities the station has to offer, including shops, cafes, and luggage storage facilities. Whether you are visiting Brussels for business or pleasure, Central Station is a must-see destination that should not be missed.

4. Diamond district

The Diamond District is a neighborhood in Antwerp, Belgium, known for its diamond trade and jewelry industry. It is one of the largest diamond centers in the world and attracts thousands of visitors every year. If you're planning a trip to Belgium, visiting the Diamond District should be on your to-do list.

Getting to the Diamond District Antwerp is located in the northern region of Belgium and is easily accessible by train, bus, and car. The city has a well-connected public transport system, with buses and trams running frequently throughout the day. The Antwerp Central Station is one of the busiest train stations in Belgium and is well-connected to major European cities like Paris, London, and Amsterdam. From the station, you can take a tram or bus to the Diamond District.

If you're coming from Brussels, you can take a train from Brussels Midi Station to Antwerp Central Station. The journey takes around 45 minutes and trains run every half hour. If you're driving, you can take the E19 motorway from Brussels to Antwerp.

The journey takes around 45 minutes, depending on traffic.

Exploring the Diamond District, The Diamond District is located in the heart of Antwerp, just a short walk from the Central Station. The district is made up of several streets, with the main one being Hoveniersstraat. Here, you'll find a variety of diamond shops and jewelry stores, each offering a unique selection of diamonds and gems.

One of the best ways to explore the Diamond District is by taking a guided tour. Several companies offer tours of the district, taking visitors behind the scenes of the diamond trade and offering an insight into the process of diamond cutting and polishing. You'll also get to see some of the most beautiful diamond creations and learn about the history of the diamond trade in Antwerp.

If you're looking to purchase a diamond or a piece of jewelry, the Diamond District is the perfect place to do so. With thousands of shops to choose from, you're sure to find the perfect piece for your collection. However, it's crucial to exercise caution and due diligence before making a purchase. Look for reputable dealers who offer a certificate of authenticity and a fair price.

In addition to diamond shopping, the Diamond District also offers a range of dining options, from traditional Belgian cuisine to international dishes. You'll find everything from cafes and bistros to fine dining restaurants, so you can enjoy a meal or a snack during your visit.

Conclusion The Diamond District in Antwerp is a must-visit destination for anyone interested in diamonds and jewelry. Whether you're looking to purchase a diamond, learn about the diamond trade, or simply explore the area, the Diamond District has something for everyone. Getting to the district is easy, with several transport options available. So, be sure to add the Diamond District to your Belgium travel itinerary and discover the beauty and glamour of the diamond world.

4. Antwerp Zoo

Antwerp Zoo, also known as the Zoo Antwerpen, is a popular attraction in Belgium. Established in 1843, it is one of the oldest zoos in the world and houses over 7,000 animals from more than 950 different species. The zoo is home to a diverse range of animals, from giraffes and elephants to sea lions and penguins.

Getting There:

Antwerp Zoo is in the heart of the city and is easily accessible by public transport, car, or bicycle.

By Public Transport:

The Antwerp Zoo is situated near the Antwerpen-Centraal railway station, making it easy to reach by train. If you're traveling from Brussels, you can take a direct train to Antwerpen-Centraal, which takes about 45 minutes. From the station, you can either walk to the zoo, which takes about 5 minutes, or take tram 6 or 12 to the stop "Antwerpen Zoo."

By Car:

If you're traveling by car, there are several parking garages nearby. The most convenient one is the Q-Park Antwerpen Zoo parking garage, located at Carnotstraat 45, 2060 Antwerpen. From there, it's just a short walk to the zoo.

By Bicycle:

Antwerp is a bike-friendly city, and you can easily reach the zoo by bicycle. There are several bike rental companies in the city, including Velo Antwerpen, which offers a bike-sharing system with several stations around the city. You can rent a bike from one of the stations and cycle to the zoo.

Attractions at Antwerp Zoo:

The Antwerp Zoo has something for everyone, from animal lovers to history buffs. The top attractions are listed below:

Elephant Enclosure: The elephant enclosure is one of the most popular attractions at the zoo. You can watch the elephants play and interact with each other in their spacious outdoor enclosure.

The Aquarium: The Antwerp Zoo's aquarium is home to over 10,000 fish and other aquatic animals. You can see sharks, rays, and sea turtles, as well as a variety of coral and other sea creatures.

The Butterfly Pavilion: The butterfly pavilion is a beautiful and tranquil space where you can walk among hundreds of colorful butterflies from around the world.

The Hippopotamus House: The hippopotamus house is a unique exhibit that allows you to watch the hippos swim and play in their spacious indoor and outdoor enclosures.

The Birdhouse: The birdhouse is home to over 100 different species of birds, including toucans, parrots, and flamingos.

The Reptile House: The reptile house is home to a diverse collection of snakes, lizards, and other reptiles from around the world.

The Great Apes: The great apes exhibit features gorillas and chimpanzees in a naturalistic habitat, where you can observe them playing, grooming, and interacting with each other.

In addition to these attractions, the Antwerp Zoo also has several restaurants, cafes, and gift shops where you can buy souvenirs and snacks.

Overall, the Antwerp Zoo is a must-visit attraction in Belgium, and its central location in Antwerp makes it easy to reach by public transport, car, or bicycle.

Welcome to Ghent

Welcome to Ghent, a city nestled in the heart of Belgium, known for its rich history, stunning architecture, vibrant cultural scene, and mouth-watering cuisine. Ghent is a true gem of Flanders, a region renowned for its medieval heritage and picturesque landscapes. With its cobblestoned streets, picturesque canals, and centuries-old buildings, Ghent is a city that exudes charm and character at every turn.

Ghent is a city of contrasts, where the old and the new blend seamlessly together. While it boasts a rich past dating back to the Middle Ages, it is also a dynamic and cosmopolitan city that is constantly evolving. Visitors can expect to find a wealth of cultural and artistic offerings, from world-class museums and galleries to cutting-edge music venues and theaters.

One of the highlights of Ghent is its stunning architecture, which ranges from Gothic to Renaissance to Baroque. The city is home to an impressive array of historical buildings and monuments, such as the imposing Gravensteen Castle, the iconic Belfry, and the majestic Saint Bavo Cathedral, which houses the world-famous Ghent Altarpiece. But Ghent is also a city that embraces modernity, with its innovative architectural designs and sustainable initiatives.

Foodies will be delighted by the diverse culinary scene in Ghent, which offers a range of delicious local specialties, including Flemish stews, waffles, and Belgian chocolates. The city is also renowned for its vibrant nightlife, with a plethora of cozy bars, trendy clubs, and live music venues.

In short, Ghent is a city that has something for everyone, whether you are interested in history, art, architecture, food, or simply soaking up the atmosphere of a charming European city. So come and explore Ghent, and discover all that this enchanting city has to offer.

5 must see attraction in Ghent.

1. Gravensteen Castle

Gravensteen Castle, also known as the Castle of the Counts, is a medieval castle located in the heart of Ghent, Belgium. This impressive fortress has a rich history, dating back to the 12th century, and is one of the most popular tourist attractions in Belgium. In this guide, we will explore the history of Gravensteen

Castle, as well as provide information on how to get there and what to expect when visiting.

History of Gravensteen Castle:

Gravensteen Castle was built in the 12th century by Philip of Alsace, the Count of Flanders. The castle was constructed to serve as the residence of the Counts of Flanders and was designed as a symbol of their power and wealth. Over the centuries, the castle underwent several modifications and additions, including the addition of a dungeon, a chapel, and a great hall.

In the 14th century, the castle's importance as a residence declined, and it was used for various purposes, including as a courthouse, a prison, and a factory. In the 19th century, the castle was scheduled for demolition, but it was saved by the efforts of the people of Ghent, who recognized its historical and cultural significance.

Today, Gravensteen Castle is a popular tourist attraction, offering visitors a glimpse into the castle's rich history and the life of the Counts of Flanders.

Getting There:

Gravensteen Castle is in the heart of Ghent, making it easily accessible by public transport or on foot. The castle is within walking distance of the city's main train station, Gent-Sint-Pieters, and is well connected by bus and tram.

By Train: Ghent-Sint-Pieters train station is well-connected to major cities in Belgium and Europe. From there, it is a 25-minute walk or a short tram ride to the castle.

By Bus: There are several bus routes that stop near the castle, including lines 3, 17, 18, and 38.

By Tram: The castle is also accessible by tram, with lines 1, 4, and 22 stopping at the Gravensteen stop.

What to Expect When Visiting:

Visitors to Gravensteen Castle can expect to see a well-preserved fortress that offers a glimpse into medieval life in Belgium. The castle is home to a museum that features exhibits on the castle's history, including its use as a courthouse, prison, and factory. The museum also features a collection of medieval weapons, armor, and torture devices.

Visitors can also explore the castle's dungeon, climb the battlements for panoramic views of the city, and visit the castle's chapel. The castle also hosts events throughout the year, including medieval-themed festivals and concerts.

Tickets for Gravensteen Castle can be purchased online or at the castle's ticket office. The castle is open daily from 9:00 am to 6:00 pm, with extended hours during the summer months.

In conclusion, Gravensteen Castle is a must-see attraction for visitors to Ghent, Belgium. With its rich history, well-preserved fortress, and panoramic views of the city, the castle offers a unique glimpse into medieval life in Flanders. Whether you are interested in history, architecture, or simply looking for an exciting day out, Gravensteen Castle is well worth a visit.

2. St. Bavo's Cathedral

St. Bavo's Cathedral, also known as the Sint-Baafskathedraal, is a breathtaking Gothic-style cathedral located in Ghent, Belgium. The cathedral is one of the most iconic landmarks in Ghent, attracting tourists from all over the world who come to marvel at its stunning architecture, priceless artwork, and religious significance.

History of St. Bavo's Cathedral:

The cathedral was originally built in the 10th century as a small Romanesque church dedicated to Saint

John the Baptist. Over time, the church was expanded and transformed into the beautiful Gothic-style cathedral we see today. The cathedral was named after Saint Bavo, a Flemish nobleman who became a Christian saint.

The cathedral has played an important role in Belgian history. In the 16th century, during the religious wars that swept across Europe, the cathedral was looted by Protestant iconoclasts who destroyed much of its artwork. Later, during the French Revolution, the cathedral was seized by the French and converted into a Temple of Reason, with many of its religious artifacts being destroyed.

However, over the years, the cathedral has been restored and many of its priceless works of art have been recovered, making it a must-see attraction for anyone visiting Ghent.

What to See at St. Bavo's Cathedral:

One of the most famous works of art housed in the cathedral is the Ghent Altarpiece, also known as The Adoration of the Mystic Lamb. The painting is an intricate masterpiece created by the Van Eyck brothers in the early 15th century and is considered one of the most important works of art in the world.

Another notable feature of the cathedral is the pulpit, which is adorned with intricate carvings and was created by the famous Flemish sculptor, Hendrik Frans Verbruggen.

Visitors can also admire the beautiful stained-glass windows, impressive organ, and the many statues and sculptures throughout the cathedral.

Getting There:

St. Bavo's Cathedral is in the heart of Ghent, making it easily accessible by public transport, bike, or on foot. If you're coming from Brussels, you can take a train from Brussels Midi station to Gent-Sint-Pieters station. From there, you can take a tram or bus to the city center.

If you're driving, there are several parking garages in the city center, including the Sint-Michielsparking garage and the Vrijdagmarkt parking garage, both of which are a short walk from the cathedral.

Opening Hours and Admission:

St. Bavo's Cathedral is open to visitors every day from 8:30 am to 6 pm (April to September) and from 8:30 am to 5 pm (October to March). Admission to the cathedral is free, but there is a small fee to see the Ghent Altarpiece.

Conclusion:

A visit to St. Bavo's Cathedral is a must for anyone visiting Ghent. With its rich history, stunning architecture, and priceless works of art, it is a true gem of Belgium's cultural heritage. Whether you're a history buff, an art lover, or just looking to soak up the beauty of one of Europe's most impressive cathedrals, St. Bavo's is sure to impress.

3. Ghent Altarpiece

The Ghent Altarpiece, also known as the Adoration of the Mystic Lamb, is one of the most famous and important works of art in Belgium, and indeed in all of Europe. It is a large and intricate polyptych, or multi-paneled altarpiece, that was painted in the 15th century by the brothers Hubert and Jan van Eyck. The altarpiece is a masterpiece of Flemish art and a testament to the skill and creativity of its creators.

Getting There:

The Ghent Altarpiece is housed in the Saint Bavo Cathedral in Ghent, Belgium. Ghent is in the Flanders region of Belgium, approximately halfway between Brussels and Bruges. There are several ways to get to Ghent from other parts of Belgium:

By Train: Ghent has two train stations, Gent-Sint-Pieters and Gent-Dampoort, which are connected to other major cities in Belgium, including Brussels, Antwerp, and Bruges. From Brussels, the journey to Ghent takes approximately 30 minutes by train.

By Car: Ghent is located near several major highways, including the E17 and E40. From Brussels, the journey to Ghent takes approximately 45 minutes by car.

By Bus: There are several bus companies that operate routes between Ghent and other cities in Belgium, including FlixBus and De Lijn.

The Ghent Altarpiece:

The Ghent Altarpiece was commissioned by the wealthy merchant and politician Joost Vijdt for his family chapel in the Saint Bavo Cathedral. The altarpiece consists of 12 panels, with six panels on each side, and measures approximately 11.5 feet by 15 feet when fully opened. The panels are arranged in two tiers, with the upper tier depicting scenes from the life of Christ and the lower tier depicting scenes from the lives of various saints and martyrs.

One of the most striking features of the Ghent Altarpiece is the central panel, which depicts the Adoration of the Mystic Lamb. This panel shows a sacrificial lamb standing on an altar, surrounded by angels, saints, and other figures. The lamb represents Christ, who is the sacrificial lamb of God in Christian theology. The panel is rich in symbolism and has inspired countless interpretations and analyses over the centuries.

The Ghent Altarpiece has had a tumultuous history, with several of its panels being stolen or damaged over the centuries. The most famous theft occurred in 1934, when the Just Judges panel was stolen and never recovered. The theft remains a mystery to this day and has inspired numerous theories and conspiracy theories.

Today, the Ghent Altarpiece is one of the most popular tourist attractions in Ghent and draws visitors from all over the world. The altarpiece is housed in the Saint Bavo Cathedral, which is a magnificent Gothic church with a long and storied history of its own.

Visiting the Ghent Altarpiece:

The Ghent Altarpiece can be viewed in the Saint Bavo Cathedral in Ghent. The cathedral is open to visitors every day, with varying hours depending on the season. Admission to the cathedral is free, but there is a fee to view the Ghent Altarpiece.

When visiting the Ghent Altarpiece, it is important to be respectful of the artwork and the cathedral. Flash photography is not permitted but other forms of photography are. Visitors should also be aware that the Ghent Altarpiece is a fragile and valuable work of art and should take care not to touch or damage it in any way.

In conclusion, the Ghent Altarpiece is an extraordinary work of art that is well worth a visit for anyone interested in art, history, or culture. With its intricate details, rich symbolism

4. Graslei and Korenlei

Graslei and Korenlei are two historic quaysides located in the heart of Ghent, Belgium. Both areas are lined with beautiful, historic buildings and offer a stunning view of the city's canals. They are popular among locals and tourists alike and offer a variety of activities, including dining, shopping, and sightseeing.

Getting to Graslei and Korenlei

Graslei and Korenlei are in the city center of Ghent, making them easily accessible by public transport or on foot. If you are arriving by train, the Ghent-Sint-

Pieters station is the main train station in Ghent, and from there you can take a tram or bus to the city center. The number 1, 4, and 24 trams and the number 3, 17, and 18 buses all stop at Korenmarkt, which is just a short walk from Graslei and Korenlei.

If you prefer to walk, it takes approximately 20 minutes to reach Graslei and Korenlei from the train station. The walk is relatively easy and takes you through the beautiful streets of Ghent. You can also rent a bike if you prefer to explore the city on two wheels.

What to do at Graslei and Korenlei

Graslei and Korenlei are best known for their historic buildings, which date back to the Middle Ages. Many of these buildings were used as guildhalls, warehouses, and trading houses during the city's heyday as a trading center. Today, they have been restored and converted into restaurants, cafes, and shops.

One of the most popular activities at Graslei and Korenlei is to simply sit and enjoy the view. There are plenty of benches along the quaysides, and you can take in the beautiful scenery of the city's canals and historic buildings. If you want to learn more about the history of the area, you can also take a guided tour or visit the nearby museums.

Food and drink are also a major attraction at Graslei and Korenlei. There are plenty of restaurants and cafes along the quaysides, serving a range of local and international cuisine. Belgian specialties, such as waffles, chocolate, and beer, are particularly popular, and you can find many places to try them in the area.

Shopping is another popular activity at Graslei and Korenlei. There are plenty of boutiques and shops selling a range of goods, including souvenirs, clothing, and jewelry. The area is particularly known for its antique shops, where you can find unique treasures and collectibles.

Conclusion

Graslei and Korenlei are two must-see attractions in Ghent, Belgium. With their stunning historic buildings, beautiful canals, and plenty of activities to enjoy, they offer something for everyone. Whether you want to enjoy a relaxing stroll, try some local cuisine, or do some shopping, Graslei and Korenlei are the perfect places to explore.

5. Ghent Floralies

Ghent Floralies is a spectacular flower show held every five years in Ghent, Belgium. It is a must-visit attraction for anyone who loves flowers, plants, and gardening. The event attracts thousands of visitors from all over the world and showcases the best of Belgian horticulture. In this guide, we will cover everything you need to know about Ghent Floralies, including how to get there and what to expect.

What is Ghent Floralies?

Ghent Floralies, also known as the Ghent Flower Show, is a grand biennial event showcasing the best of Belgian floriculture. It features a wide range of plants and flowers, from traditional favorites to rare and exotic specimens. The event takes place over a 10-day period, during which time visitors can enjoy stunning floral displays, live entertainment, and other activities.

The history of Ghent Floralies dates to 1809 when it was first held in Saint Peter's Square in Ghent. Since then, the event has grown and popularity, attracting visitors from all over the world. It is now one of the largest and most prestigious flowers shows in Europe.

When are Ghent Floralies held?

Ghent Floralies are held every five years, typically in the months of April and May. The exact dates vary, so it is best to check the event's official website for the latest information. The event runs for 10 days, from 8:00 a.m. to 7:00 p.m. daily.

How to get to Ghent Floralies

Getting to Ghent Floralies is relatively easy, as Ghent is well-connected to other cities in Belgium and Europe. Here are a few of the most popular transportation options:

By Train: Ghent has excellent train connections with other Belgian cities and major European cities, including Paris, London, and Amsterdam. The main railway station in Ghent is Gent-Sint-Pieters, which is located about 2.5 kilometers from the city center. From the station, you can take a tram, bus or taxi to the event venue.

By Car: If you are driving to Ghent Floralies, there are several parking options available in and around the city center. However, it is worth noting that traffic in Ghent can be heavy, especially during peak hours.

By Bus: Ghent has an extensive network of buses that connect different parts of the city. There are also regional buses that connect Ghent with other towns and cities in the region. You can take a bus to the event venue from the city center.

What to expect at Ghent Floralies

Ghent Floralies is a grand event that attracts visitors from all over the world. Here are some of the things you can expect to see and do at the event:

Stunning Floral Displays: The main attraction of Ghent Floralies is the stunning floral displays. The event showcases a wide range of plants and flowers, including rare and exotic specimens. There are several indoor and outdoor displays that are sure to take your breath away.

Live Entertainment: Ghent Floralies also features live entertainment, including music, dance, and other performances. There are several stages set up around the event venue where you can enjoy the performances.

Food and Drink: There are several food and drink stalls at Ghent Floralies where you can sample local cuisine and drinks. From traditional Belgian waffles to craft beers, there is something for everyone.

Shopping: If you love gardening and plants, you will love the shopping opportunities at Ghent Floralies.

There are several stalls selling plants, flowers, and gardening accessories.

Conclusion

Ghent Floralies is a must-visit attraction for anyone who loves flowers, plants, and gardening. The event showcases the best of Belgian horticulture and attracts.

Welcome to Bruges

Welcome to Bruges, one of the most picturesque and charming cities in Belgium! Bruges, also known as the "Venice of the North," is a city with a rich history and architecture that dates to the medieval period. The city is in the northwest part of Belgium, in the province of West Flanders, and is a popular destination for tourists from all over the world.

Getting to Bruges:

There are several ways to get to Bruges. The city is well-connected by road, rail, and air. If you are flying, the closest airport to Bruges is Brussels Airport, which is approximately 110 km away. You can take a train or bus from the airport to Bruges. If you are coming by train, the Bruges train station is in the city center, and it is well-connected to other major cities in Belgium and Europe.

Things to see and do in Bruges:

Markt Square: This is the central square of Bruges and is surrounded by impressive buildings and architecture. You can visit the Belfry Tower, which offers a stunning panoramic view of the city.

Canals: Bruges is known for its network of canals, which give it the nickname "Venice of the North." You can take a boat tour of the canals to see the city from a different perspective.

Basilica of the Holy Blood: This is a 12th-century basilica that is home to a relic believed to be the blood of Jesus Christ. The relic is housed in a crystal vial and is on display to the public.

Groeningemuseum: This museum is home to a vast collection of Flemish and Belgian art, including works by famous artists such as Jan van Eyck, Hieronymus Bosch, and Hans Memling.

Chocolate and beer: Belgium is known for its chocolate and beer, and Bruges is no exception. You can visit one of the many chocolate shops in the city to sample some of the best chocolate in the world. You can also try some of the local beers, which are brewed in the traditional Belgian style.

Lace making: Bruges is known for its lace making, which is a traditional craft that has been passed down for generations. You can visit one of the lace-making workshops in the city to see how this intricate craft is done.

Where to stay:

There are several accommodation options in Bruges, ranging from luxury hotels to budget-friendly hostels. If you want to stay in the heart of the city, then the Markt Square area is a good option. You can also find accommodation options in other parts of the city, such as the Old Town, which is known for its historic architecture.

When to visit:

Bruges is a year-round destination, but the best time to visit is between March and October, when the weather is mild, and the city is bustling with tourists. If you want to avoid the crowds, then it is best to visit in the shoulder seasons, which are April-May and September-October.

In conclusion, Bruges is a must-visit destination for anyone traveling to Belgium. The city is filled with history, culture, and charm, and there is something for everyone to enjoy. From the beautiful canals to the delicious chocolate and beer, Bruges is sure to leave you with

5 must see attractions in Bruges.

1. Historic Centre of Bruges

The Historic Centre of Bruges is a UNESCO World Heritage Site located in the charming city of Bruges, Belgium. Known for its well-preserved medieval architecture, picturesque canals, and delicious chocolates, Bruges is a must-visit destination for anyone traveling to Belgium. In this guide, we'll cover everything you need to know about visiting the Historic Centre of Bruges, including how to get there, what to see and do, and where to stay.

Getting There

Bruges is in the northwest corner of Belgium, approximately 100 kilometers from Brussels. The easiest way to get to Bruges is by train from Brussels or other major cities in Belgium. The train station in Bruges is located just outside the city center, and it's a short walk or bus ride to the Historic Centre.

If you're traveling from outside Belgium, the nearest international airport is Brussels Airport. From there, you can take a train or bus to Bruges, or rent a car and drive yourself.

What to See and Do

The Historic Centre of Bruges is a small area, but it's packed with sights and attractions. Here are some of the must-see sights in Bruges:

Markt Square: This is the heart of Bruges, a bustling square surrounded by medieval buildings and home to the iconic Belfry Tower. There are also plenty of restaurants, cafes, and shops in the square.

Belfry Tower: Climb the 366 steps to the top of the Belfry Tower for a stunning view of Bruges.

Church of Our Lady: This stunning Gothic church is home to a famous sculpture of Madonna and Child by Michelangelo.

Groeningemuseum: This art museum features works by Flemish painters such as Jan van Eyck and Hans Memling.

Canals of Bruges: Take a boat tour of the canals to see the city from a different perspective.

Choco-Story: Learn about the history of chocolate and sample some delicious Belgian chocolate at this museum.

Where to Stay

There are plenty of accommodation options in Bruges, ranging from budget hostels to luxury hotels. If you want to stay in the heart of the Historic Centre, look for hotels or guesthouses near Markt Square. Some of the top-rated hotels in Bruges include the Hotel Heritage, the Pand Hotel, and the Hotel Dukes' Palace.

Final Thoughts

The Historic Centre of Bruges is a beautiful and charming destination that should be on every traveler's itinerary when visiting Belgium. With its medieval architecture, picturesque canals, and delicious chocolate, Bruges has something for everyone. Whether you're interested in art and history, or just want to relax and enjoy the scenery, Bruges is a must-visit destination.

2. Belfry of Bruges

The Belfry of Bruges is one of the most iconic landmarks in Belgium. This medieval tower is in the heart of Bruges, a charming city that is often referred to as the "Venice of the North" due to its network of canals and picturesque architecture. The Belfry is a UNESCO World Heritage Site and a must-visit attraction for anyone traveling to Belgium.

History of the Belfry of Bruges

The Belfry of Bruges was first built in the 13th century and has undergone several renovations and additions over the centuries. Originally used as a watchtower for the city, it later became a symbol of the city's prosperity and independence. The tower also housed the city's treasury and archives.

The tower has had a tumultuous history, including several fires, lightning strikes, and even an explosion in the 15th century. It has been rebuilt and restored multiple times, with the most recent renovation taking place in the 19th century.

Today, the Belfry of Bruges stands at 83 meters tall and is the tallest structure in the city. Visitors can climb the tower's 366 steps for stunning views of Bruges and the surrounding countryside.

Getting to the Belfry of Bruges

Bruges is easily accessible by train from major cities in Belgium, including Brussels, Ghent, and Antwerp. From the train station, visitors can take a short walk or a taxi to the city center. The Belfry is located in the Markt, the central square of Bruges, and is within walking distance of many other attractions in the city.

For those driving, there are several parking garages located in the city center, although parking can be quite expensive. Alternatively, visitors can park for free at the train station and take a short walk or bus ride into the city center.

Visiting the Belfry of Bruges

The Belfry of Bruges is open to visitors daily from 9:30 am to 6 pm, although hours may vary during holidays and peak tourist season. Admission to the tower is €12 for adults, €10 for students and seniors, and €5 for children ages 6-12. Little ones under six enter free of charge.

Visitors should be prepared for a steep climb up the tower's narrow staircase. The climb can be challenging, particularly for those with mobility issues or a fear of heights. But the ascent is totally worthwhile because of the breathtaking views at the top.

In addition to the tower itself, visitors can also explore the Belfry's museum, which features exhibits on the tower's history and the city's bell-ringing tradition. The museum is located on the lower levels of the tower and is included with the price of admission.

.

The Belfry of Bruges is a must-visit attraction for anyone traveling to Belgium. This iconic tower offers stunning views of the city and a glimpse into Bruges' rich history. While the climb up the tower can be challenging, it is well worth the effort for the breathtaking views from the top. With its central location in the heart of Bruges, the Belfry is easily accessible by train or car, making it a convenient stop on any Belgium travel itinerary.

3. Markt

Belgium is a small yet culturally diverse country that is home to some of Europe's most charming towns and cities, including its capital Brussels. One of the most appealing aspects of traveling to Belgium is the ease of getting around and exploring the various markets, including the famous Christmas markets, which are held throughout the country.

Markets in Belgium are a significant part of the country's culture and are always lively and bustling with people. They offer an excellent opportunity to sample the local delicacies, buy handmade goods, and immerse yourself in the vibrant atmosphere.

Here are some of the most popular markets in Belgium that you can visit during your trip:

Grand-Place Market, Brussels: The Grand-Place in Brussels is the city's central square and home to a daily market selling souvenirs, flowers, and local foods. The market is surrounded by stunning architecture, including the Town Hall, making it a great place to wander and take in the sights.

Bruges Christmas Market: Bruges, often referred to as the 'Venice of the North,' is a picturesque city that comes alive during the festive season. The Bruges Christmas Market is one of the most popular markets in Belgium, with an ice-skating rink, a Ferris wheel, and numerous stalls selling handcrafted goods and local foods.

Antwerp's Sunday Market: Held every Sunday, Antwerp's market is a haven for vintage and antique lovers. Here you can find everything from retro furniture to vintage clothing and accessories, making it the perfect place to hunt for unique souvenirs.

Liege Sunday Market: Another Sunday market that is worth a visit is Liege's Marche de la Batte. It's one of the largest markets in Europe, with over 500 stalls selling everything from fresh produce to clothes, shoes, and household goods.

Getting to the markets in Belgium is easy, with excellent public transport links connecting the major cities and towns. You can also hire a car or take a taxi if you prefer.

If you're flying into Belgium, Brussels International Airport is the main entry point. From there, you can take a train or bus to your chosen destination.

Belgium's train system is one of the most efficient and reliable in Europe, with regular services running between major cities and towns. The Belgian Railways website provides up-to-date information on train times and fares, making it easy to plan your journey.

Alternatively, you can take a bus, which is often cheaper than the train. Flixbus is a popular bus operator that runs services throughout Belgium and Europe.

In conclusion, exploring the markets in Belgium is a must-do activity during your trip. From antiques to local foods and souvenirs, there is something for everyone. Getting there is easy, with excellent public transport links connecting the major cities and towns, making it easy to explore this fascinating country.

4.Groeninge museum

The Groeningemuseum is a renowned museum located in Bruges, Belgium. It is home to an impressive collection of Flemish and Belgian art from the medieval period to the present day. The museum's name refers to the medieval Groeninge battlefield, where a battle was fought between the Flemish townspeople and French knights in 1302.

The Groeningemuseum is an excellent destination for art lovers and history buffs who want to learn about Flemish and Belgian art. It has an extensive collection of paintings, sculptures, and drawings from artists such as Jan van Eyck, Hans Memling, Hieronymus Bosch, and Pieter Bruegel the Elder.

The museum's collection is divided into six different rooms, each showcasing art from different periods. The first room exhibits paintings from the 14th and 15th centuries, including works by Jan van Eyck and Hans Memling. The second room displays art from the 16th century, with works by Pieter Bruegel the Elder, among others. The third room is dedicated to the 17th century, and features paintings by Flemish Baroque artists such as Anthony van Dyck and Peter Paul Rubens. The fourth room showcases art from the 18th and 19th centuries, including works by James Ensor and Gustave van de Woestijne. The fifth room is dedicated to modern art from the 20th century, featuring works by artists such as Permeke and Magritte. The sixth and final room displays contemporary art.

Getting to the Groeningemuseum is relatively easy, as it is in the historic center of Bruges. The museum is just a short walk away from the city's central market square, which is easily accessible by public transportation. Visitors can take the train to Bruges station, which is located just outside the city center. From there, they can take a bus or taxi to the museum or walk for approximately 20 minutes.

If you prefer to travel by car, there are several parking garages located in the city center. However, visitors should be aware that parking can be challenging in Bruges, particularly during peak tourist season.

From Tuesday through Sunday, 9:30 am to 5:00 pm, the museum is open. The cost of admission varies by age and place of residence. Visitors can purchase tickets in advance online or at the museum entrance.

In conclusion, the Groeningemuseum is an excellent destination for art lovers and history buffs who want to learn about Flemish and Belgian art. With its impressive collection of paintings, sculptures, and drawings from medieval times to the present day, the museum offers a fascinating journey through Belgium's artistic heritage. Getting there is relatively easy, with multiple options for public transportation, and ample parking available for those traveling by car.

5. Chocolate shops and museums

Belgium is known as the chocolate capital of the world, with a long history of producing high-quality chocolate. In fact, chocolate-making is considered an art form in Belgium, and visitors to the country can experience this art first-hand by visiting chocolate shops and museums throughout the country.

Chocolate Shops

Belgium is home to countless chocolate shops, ranging from small family-run businesses to large luxury stores. Some of the most well-known chocolate shops in Belgium include:

Neuhaus: Founded in 1857, Neuhaus is one of the oldest chocolate shops in Belgium. Their signature chocolate is the praline, which was invented by the founder of the shop.

Leonidas: Leonidas is a Belgian chocolate brand that was founded in 1913. They are known for their high-quality pralines and truffles, which are made with fresh ingredients and no preservatives.

Godiva: Godiva is a luxury chocolate brand that was founded in Brussels in 1926. Their chocolates are made with high-quality cocoa beans and are known for their smooth and creamy texture.

Pierre Marcolini: Pierre Marcolini is a renowned chocolatier who has won numerous awards for his chocolate creations. His chocolates are made with high-quality ingredients and are known for their unique flavor combinations.

Wittamer: Wittamer is a family-run chocolate shop that has been in business since 1910. They are known for their high-quality chocolates and pastries, which are made with fresh ingredients and no preservatives.

Chocolate Museums

In addition to chocolate shops, Belgium is also home to several chocolate museums that offer visitors an opportunity to learn about the history of chocolate-making in the country. Some of the most popular chocolate museums in Belgium include:

Choco-Story: Choco-Story is a chocolate museum that is in Brussels. It offers visitors an interactive experience that includes a guided tour of the museum, a demonstration of chocolate-making techniques, and a tasting of different types of chocolate.

Chocolate Nation: Chocolate Nation is a chocolate museum that is in Antwerp. It offers visitors an immersive experience that includes a guided tour of the museum, a demonstration of chocolate-making techniques, and a tasting of different types of chocolate.

The Chocolate Line: The Chocolate Line is a chocolate shop that also offers visitors a chance to learn about chocolate-making. They offer workshops where visitors can make their own chocolates and learn about the history of chocolate in Belgium.

Getting There

Belgium is a small country, which makes it easy to travel between different cities and towns. Visitors can get to chocolate shops and museums in Belgium by train, bus, or car.

Train: Belgium has a comprehensive train network that connects cities and towns throughout the country. The train is a convenient and affordable way to travel, and it is particularly useful for visitors who want to travel between Brussels and other cities such as Bruges or Antwerp.

Bus: Buses are another option for visitors who want to travel between cities and towns in Belgium. They are less expensive than trains, but they can take longer and are less comfortable.

Car: Visitors who want more flexibility and independence can rent a car to travel between chocolate shops and museums in Belgium. This is particularly useful for visitors who want to explore more remote areas of the country.

In conclusion, Belgium is a chocolate-lover's paradise, with countless chocolate shops and museums to explore. Whether you want to learn about the history of chocolate-making or simply indulge in some of the world's best chocolate, Belgium is the perfect destination. Visitors can easily get to chocolate shops and museums in Belgium by train, bus, or car, making it a convenient and accessible destination for all.

Welcome to Leuven

Welcome to Leuven, a beautiful city in Belgium that boasts of rich cultural heritage and a vibrant student life. Located in the Flemish Region, Leuven is renowned for its picturesque architecture, friendly locals, and delicious Belgian cuisine. Whether you're an avid traveler, a foodie, or a history buff, Leuven has something for everyone.

Getting to Leuven is quite easy, as it is only a short distance away from Brussels, the capital city of

Belgium. Visitors can travel by train or bus, with both options taking around 30 minutes to reach Leuven. If you prefer to drive, it's also possible to rent a car and drive to the city.

One of the must-see attractions in Leuven is the Grote Markt, the city's central square. The square is surrounded by beautiful historic buildings, such as the Town Hall, which dates to the 15th century. Visitors can also see the impressive St. Peter's Church, which is over 500 years old and houses a range of beautiful paintings and sculptures.

Leuven is also home to the stunning University Library, a UNESCO World Heritage Site. The library is renowned for its striking architecture and beautiful interiors, and visitors can take guided tours to explore its rich history and unique features.

For those who love beer, Leuven is the perfect destination. The city is home to the famous Stella Artois brewery, which has been producing beer since

1926. Visitors can take a guided tour of the brewery, learn about the beer-making process, and even taste some of the delicious brews.

If you're interested in exploring the natural beauty of the area, Leuven is surrounded by stunning countryside and picturesque villages. Visitors can take a bike tour of the area, or even go on a hot air balloon ride to see the city from above.

For food lovers, Leuven has a range of delicious Belgian cuisine to offer. The city is renowned for its waffles, chocolate, and beer, and visitors can sample these delights in many of the local cafes and restaurants. Some of the most popular dishes include moules frites (mussels and fries), stoofvlees (beef stew), and of course, the famous Belgian fries.

In terms of accommodation, Leuven has a range of options to suit all budgets. There are several luxurious hotels, as well as budget-friendly hostels and bed and breakfasts. Visitors can also choose to stay in the city center or in the surrounding countryside, depending on their preferences.

Overall, Leuven is a fantastic destination for anyone visiting Belgium. With its rich cultural heritage, vibrant student life, and stunning natural beauty, there is something for everyone in this charming city. Whether you're interested in history, food, or adventure, Leuven has it all. So, pack your bags and get ready for an unforgettable trip to this beautiful part of Belgium.

5 must see attractions in Leuven.

1. Town Hall

Leuven Town Hall is a historic landmark located in the center of Leuven, a charming university town in Belgium. This impressive building is considered one of the finest examples of Gothic architecture in the country and is a must-visit attraction for anyone visiting Leuven.

History of Leuven Town Hall:

The construction of Leuven Town Hall began in 1439 and was completed in 1469. The building served as the seat of local government and as a symbol of the town's prosperity and power. The design of the town hall was inspired by the town halls of Brussels and Bruges, but it also incorporated elements of local Brabant Gothic architecture.

Over the centuries, the town hall underwent several renovations and additions. In the 19th century, a new façade was added to the building, which gave it a more neoclassical look. The building was heavily damaged during World War II but was fully restored in the post-war period.

Today, the town hall is still used for its original purpose as the seat of local government. It also serves as a popular venue for events and concerts.

What to see at Leuven Town Hall:
The most striking feature of the town hall is its ornate façade, which is decorated with more than 200 statues of famous historical and mythological figures. The façade also features intricate carvings

and ornate details, including Gothic arches and spires.

Inside, visitors can explore the various rooms and halls of the town hall, including the Council Chamber, where local government meetings are held. The Council Chamber is decorated with beautiful tapestries and paintings and features an impressive ceiling with intricate carvings and paintings.

Another highlight of the town hall is the Wedding Hall, which is used for civil wedding ceremonies. The hall is decorated with beautiful frescoes and features a stunning vaulted ceiling.

Getting to Leuven Town Hall:

Leuven is easily accessible by train from Brussels, which is only 20 minutes away. There are also direct trains to Leuven from other major Belgian cities, including Antwerp, Ghent, and Bruges.

Once you arrive in Leuven, the town hall is located in the heart of the city center, just a short walk from the train station. You can also take a bus or taxi to the town hall if you prefer.

Overall, Leuven Town Hall is a must-visit attraction for anyone traveling to Belgium. Its stunning Gothic architecture and rich history make it a truly unique and memorable experience.

2. St. Peter's Church

St. Peter's Church is a magnificent Gothic church located in the heart of Leuven, a vibrant and charming city in Belgium. It is one of the most popular tourist attractions in the city and is known for its impressive architecture, rich history, and stunning artwork.

History of St. Peter's Church:

The history of St. Peter's Church dates to the 14th century when it was built as a parish church. Over the centuries, the church underwent several renovations and expansions, with the most significant ones taking place in the 15th and 16th centuries when it was transformed into a Gothic masterpiece.

During the French Revolution, the church was looted and damaged, and it wasn't until the 19th century that it was restored to its former glory. Today, St. Peter's Church is considered one of the finest examples of Gothic architecture in Belgium and is a testament to the city's rich cultural heritage.

Architecture and Artwork:

One of the most striking features of St. Peter's Church is its towering spire, which rises to a height of over 90 meters and can be seen from almost any part of the city. The church's facade is adorned with intricate carvings and sculptures, and its interior is equally impressive, with soaring arches, stained glass windows, and a magnificent organ.

The church is also home to several important works of art, including the famous Last Supper painting by Flemish master Dieric Bouts. Other notable artworks include the stunning Baroque pulpit, the 15th-century triptych altar, and the 16th-century choir stalls.

Getting to St. Peter's Church:

St. Peter's Church is in the heart of Leuven, making it easily accessible on foot or by public transport. The church is just a short walk from the city center and is located near several other popular attractions, such as the Leuven Town Hall and the Grote Markt.

If you're traveling to Leuven from Brussels, the easiest way to get to St. Peter's Church is by train. Trains run regularly between Brussels and Leuven, and the journey takes just 20-30 minutes. From the Leuven train station, it's a short walk to the city center and St. Peter's Church.

If you're driving to Leuven, there are several public parking lots located near the city center, including the Heilig Hart parking garage, which is just a few minutes' walk from St. Peter's Church.

In conclusion, St. Peter's Church is a must-visit destination for anyone traveling to Leuven or Belgium. Its stunning Gothic architecture, rich history, and impressive artwork make it a truly unforgettable experience. With its central location and easy accessibility, it's easy to see why St. Peter's Church is one of the most popular tourist attractions in the city.

3. Old Market Square

Old Market Square, also known as Grote Markt, is the central square in the historic heart of many Belgian cities. The square is often the hub of cultural events and activities, making it an essential stop for travelers interested in exploring the local culture. In this guide, we will focus on the Old Market Square in Brussels, Belgium, and how to get there.

\About Old Market Square in Brussels

Located in the center of Brussels, Old Market Square is a beautiful square that dates to the 15th century. It is surrounded by stunning medieval architecture, including the famous Brussels City Hall and the beautiful Maison du Roi. The square is also home to many cafes, restaurants, and bars, making it an ideal place to stop for a meal or a drink.

The square is particularly stunning at night when the buildings are lit up and the atmosphere is buzzing with activity. Visitors can expect to find street performers, musicians, and artists, adding to the lively atmosphere of the square.

How to Get to Old Market Square in Brussels

There are several ways to get to Old Market Square in Brussels, depending on where you are coming from.

By Train If you are coming from another part of Belgium or from a nearby country, such as France or the Netherlands, you may be able to take a train to Brussels Central Station. From there, it is a short walk to Old Market Square.

By Bus or Tram Brussels has an excellent public transportation system, including buses and trams. Visitors can take the tram to the Grote Markt stop, which is located right in the heart of Old Market Square.

By Car If you are driving to Brussels, you can park your car in one of the many public parking garages located in the city center. From there, it is a short walk to Old Market Square.

Tips for Visiting Old Market Square in Brussels

Here are some tips to help you make the most of your visit to Old Market Square in Brussels:

Plan to visit in the evening: The square comes alive at night with street performers, musicians, and artists. It's a great place to experience the lively atmosphere of Brussels.

Try the local cuisine: There are many restaurants and cafes around the square serving traditional Belgian cuisine, such as mussels, fries, and beer.

Take a guided tour: A guided tour can provide insight into the history and culture of the square and the surrounding area.

Visit during a festival: The square is often the hub of cultural festivals and events, including the famous Brussels Christmas market.

Take a photo with the Manneken Pis: The famous statue of the peeing boy is located just a short walk from Old Market Square and is a popular tourist attraction.

In conclusion, Old Market Square in Brussels is a must-visit destination for travelers interested in exploring the local culture and history of Belgium. With its stunning medieval architecture, lively atmosphere, and delicious cuisine, it is a great place to spend an evening or a whole day. Getting there is easy, and there are plenty of activities and events to keep visitors entertained.

4. University of Leuven

The University of Leuven, also known as KU Leuven, is one of the oldest and most prestigious universities in Europe. Founded in 1425, it is located in the historic city of Leuven, Belgium, and has a rich history of academic excellence and innovation.

Getting to Leuven

Leuven is conveniently located in the heart of Belgium, with excellent transport links to the rest of the country and beyond. Here are some of the best ways to get to Leuven:

By Plane: The closest airport to Leuven is Brussels Airport, which is located just 25km away. From there, you can take a train or bus to Leuven, which takes around 15-20 minutes.

By Train: Leuven is well-connected by train to other major cities in Belgium and Europe. The main train station in Leuven is located in the city center, making it easy to get around once you arrive.

By Bus: There are also several bus services that run to and from Leuven, making it easy to get there from other parts of Belgium and Europe.

The University of Leuven

The University of Leuven is a world-renowned institution that offers a wide range of academic programs across a variety of disciplines. It is known for its research excellence and innovative teaching methods, and has produced many notable alumni over the years, including Nobel laureates and world leaders.

The university is spread out across several campuses in and around the city of Leuven, each with its own unique character and atmosphere. The main campus is located in the city center, and is home to many of the university's faculties and departments. Other campuses include the Arenberg campus, which is known for its science and engineering programs, and the Health Sciences campus, which focuses on medical research and education.

Things to Do in Leuven

Leuven is a beautiful and historic city that is well worth exploring. Here are some of the top things to do in Leuven:

Visit the Grote Markt: This historic square is the heart of Leuven, and is surrounded by beautiful buildings and cafes. It's a great place to relax and soak up the atmosphere.

Explore the Begijnhof: This UNESCO World Heritage Site is a beautiful and peaceful enclave that was once home to a community of religious women. It's a great place to take a walk and admire the traditional Flemish architecture.

Visit the M - Museum Leuven: This modern art museum is located in the heart of Leuven, and features a wide range of contemporary art from Belgium and beyond.

5. Leuven Beer Weekend

Leuven Beer Weekend is an annual event held in the city of Leuven, Belgium. The event takes place every year during the first weekend of September, and it is one of the most important beer festivals in Belgium. If you're a beer lover and planning a trip to Belgium, Leuven Beer Weekend is definitely an event you don't want to miss.

The festival attracts thousands of visitors from all over the world, who come to experience the best of Belgian beer culture.

It's a celebration of the rich history and tradition of Belgian brewing, and it showcases some of the finest beers produced by Belgian breweries.

During the Leuven Beer Weekend, visitors can sample a wide range of beers from over 40 breweries across the country. Some of the breweries that participate in the festival include Duvel, Westmalle, and Rochefort, among others. Visitors can also attend masterclasses and workshops on brewing techniques and beer styles, as well as take part in guided tours of local breweries.

One of the highlights of the festival is the "Beer Parade", which takes place on Saturday afternoon. During the parade, a procession of brewery carts, floats, and marching bands make their way through the city, accompanied by locals and visitors alike. The parade is a colorful and lively event that showcases the diversity and richness of Belgian beer culture.

In addition to the beer tasting and the parade, there are also numerous food stalls and vendors selling traditional Belgian food and snacks. Visitors can try classic Belgian dishes like moules-frites (mussels and fries), carbonnade flamande (beef stew), and waffles.

The Leuven Beer Weekend is also a great opportunity to explore the city of Leuven itself. Located just 30 minutes from Brussels, Leuven is a charming university town with a rich history and a lively atmosphere. Visitors can explore the city's many historic buildings and landmarks, including the Gothic-style St. Peter's Church and the picturesque Grote Markt square.

Overall, the Leuven Beer Weekend is a fantastic event that offers visitors a unique opportunity to experience the best of Belgian beer culture. Whether you're a seasoned beer aficionado or simply looking to explore the rich history and traditions of Belgian brewing, this festival is definitely worth a visit.

Accommodations in Flanders

Flanders is a region in the northern part of Belgium known for its rich history, stunning architecture, delicious cuisine, and warm hospitality. When it comes to accommodation, Flanders has plenty of options to suit every budget and preference. From luxurious hotels to cozy B&Bs and affordable hostels, you'll find something to fit your needs. Here are some of the most popular accommodation options in Flanders:

Hotels:

Flanders has a wide range of hotels, from budget-friendly options to high-end luxury properties. Many hotels are located in historic buildings, offering a unique and authentic experience. Some of the top hotels in Flanders include Hotel Heritage in Bruges, which is housed in a 19th-century mansion and features elegant rooms and a gourmet restaurant, and the Grand Hotel Brussels in Brussels, which boasts a prime location near the Grand Place and stylish rooms with modern amenities.

Bed and Breakfasts:

If you're looking for a more intimate and personal experience, staying in a bed and breakfast might be the perfect choice. Flanders has many charming B&Bs located in historic buildings and cozy neighborhoods. Some popular options include the B&B Huis Koning in Ghent, which is housed in a 19th-century mansion and features stylish rooms and a lush garden, and the B&B Aquabello in Bruges, which offers elegant rooms with views of the canal and a delicious breakfast buffet.

Hostels:

For budget-conscious travelers, hostels are a great option. Flanders has many affordable hostels located in convenient locations, making them ideal for backpackers and solo travelers. Some of the top hostels in Flanders include the Brussels Hostel in Brussels, which is located near the Grand Place and offers clean and comfortable dorms and private rooms, and the Antwerp Central Youth Hostel in Antwerp, which is housed in a historic building and features a large common area and a rooftop terrace.

Holiday Rentals:

If you're traveling with a group or looking for more space and privacy, renting a holiday home or apartment might be the way to go. Flanders has many holiday rentals available, ranging from cozy apartments to spacious villas. Some of the top rental properties in Flanders include the Antwerp City Loft in Antwerp, which is a stylish and spacious loft apartment in the heart of the city, and the Villa Belle Epoque in Ostend, which is a beautiful villa with a large garden and sea views.

Camping:

If you enjoy camping and the great outdoors, Flanders has many campsites to choose from. Whether you're traveling in a tent or a caravan, you'll find plenty of options for camping in Flanders. Some of the top campsites include the Kompas Camping Nieuwpoort in Nieuwpoort, which is located near the beach and features modern facilities and activities for all ages, and the Camping Houtum in Kasterlee, which is nestled in a beautiful forest and offers a peaceful and natural setting.

In conclusion, Flanders has a wide range of accommodations to suit every budget and preference. Whether you're looking for a luxurious hotel or a budget-friendly hostel, you'll find plenty of options in this charming region of Belgium. Whatever your choice, you can be sure that you'll receive a warm welcome and enjoy an unforgettable stay in Flanders.

10 must try Food and drink in Flanders.

Flanders, the northern region of Belgium, is a culinary paradise for foodies from all over the world. From hearty stews and comforting soups to mouth-watering chocolates and world-class beers, Flanders has it all. Here are ten must-try food and drink experiences for your next visit to this gastronomic region.

Belgian Waffles

No trip to Belgium is complete without trying the iconic Belgian waffle. Crispy on the outside and soft on the inside, these delicious treats can be enjoyed with toppings like whipped cream, fresh fruit, and Belgian chocolate.

Frites

Belgian fries, or "frites", are world-renowned for their crispy exterior and soft interior. These tasty snacks are traditionally served in a paper cone and come with a variety of dipping sauces such as mayonnaise, ketchup, or andalouse sauce.

Waterzooi

Waterzooi is a hearty Flemish stew made with fish or chicken, vegetables, and cream. This warming dish is perfect for chilly days and is often served with crusty bread for dipping.

Carbonnade Flamande

Carbonnade Flamande is a rich beef stew made with beer, onions, and spices. The beef is slow-cooked until it is tender and the beer adds a unique depth of flavor to the dish.

Flemish Asparagus

Asparagus is a popular vegetable in Flanders, and the region is known for producing some of the best quality asparagus in Europe. Asparagus is often served with melted butter and a poached egg.

Speculoos

Speculoos are traditional Belgian spiced biscuits made with cinnamon, ginger, and cloves. These delicious biscuits are often served with coffee or tea and can also be used as a base for cheesecake or as a topping for ice cream.

Belgian Chocolate

Belgium is famous for its high-quality chocolate, and Flanders is no exception. Whether you prefer milk, dark, or white chocolate, there is a wide range of flavors and textures to choose from.

Belgian Beer

Belgium is home to some of the best beer in the world, with over 1500 varieties to choose from. Whether you prefer a fruity lambic or a rich, malty Trappist ale, there is a beer for every taste.

Jenever

Jenever is a traditional Belgian spirit made from malt wine, juniper berries, and other botanicals. This strong drink is often enjoyed as an aperitif or digestif and is a must-try for anyone who loves strong, flavorful spirits.

Flemish Red Ale

Flemish Red Ale is a unique beer style that is only produced in Flanders. This sour, fruity beer is aged in oak barrels for several years, giving it a complex and interesting flavor profile.

In conclusion, Flanders is a paradise for foodies and drink enthusiasts. From sweet treats like Belgian waffles and Speculoos to savory stews like Waterzooi and Carbonnade Flamande, there is a wide range of flavors and dishes to explore. And, of course, no visit to Flanders is complete without trying the famous Belgian chocolate, beer, and Jenever.

Belgian waffle

Events and festivals in Flanders

Flanders, the Dutch-speaking region of Belgium, is home to a variety of events and festivals throughout the year. From cultural celebrations to culinary fairs, there is something for everyone to enjoy. Here are some of the top events and festivals to check out in Flanders:

Gentse Feesten: The Ghent Festival is one of the largest cultural events in Europe, attracting more than 2 million visitors each year. The festival takes place over 10 days in July and features music, theater, street performances, and plenty of food and drink.

Tomorrowland: Held in the town of Boom in late July, Tomorrowland is one of the world's largest electronic music festivals, featuring top DJs from around the globe. The festival's elaborate stages and light shows create a truly immersive experience for attendees.

Brussels Christmas Market: The Christmas market in Brussels is a magical winter wonderland, with stalls selling gifts, sweets, and hot drinks. The market is in the Grand Place, which is decorated with a huge Christmas tree and a light show.

Ommegang: This historical reenactment takes place in Brussels in early July and commemorates the entry of Emperor Charles V into the city in 1549. The event features a parade of actors in medieval costume and culminates in a mock battle in the Grand Place.

Antwerp Fashion Weekend: Held twice a year in March and September, Antwerp Fashion Weekend is a celebration of the city's fashion industry. The event features fashion shows, designer exhibitions, and pop-up shops.

Leuven Beer Festival: This annual beer festival in Leuven takes place in late April and features more than 150 different Belgian beers from over 40 breweries. Visitors can sample a variety of beers and learn about the brewing process from experts.

Bruges Chocolate Festival: This festival takes place in early February and celebrates the city's most famous export: chocolate. The festival features chocolate-making demonstrations, tastings, and competitions.

Flanders International Film Festival: This film festival takes place in Ghent in October and is one of the most important film events in Belgium. The festival showcases a selection of international films and hosts Q&A sessions with directors and actors.

Rock Werchter: Held in late June, Rock Werchter is one of Europe's biggest rock music festivals, with top acts from around the world. The festival takes place in Werchter, a small town near Brussels, and features multiple stages and a camping area.

Tournai Procession of the Holy Blood: This religious procession takes place in the city of Tournai on Ascension Day and commemorates the arrival of a relic believed to be a piece of the Holy Blood. The procession features actors in historical costume and culminates in a ceremony at the cathedral.

These are just a few of the many events and festivals that take place in Flanders throughout the year. Whether you're a music lover, a foodie, or a history buff, there is sure to be something to pique your interest in this vibrant region of Belgium.

CHAPTER 3

Welcome to Wallonia

Welcome to Wallonia, the French-speaking southern region of Belgium.

Wallonia is known for its charming small towns, rolling hills, and rich cultural heritage. From its delicious food and drink to its stunning architecture and historical landmarks, Wallonia is an excellent destination for travelers looking to experience the best of Belgium.

Getting to Wallonia is easy, as the region is well-connected by train, bus, and road networks.

Charleroi and Liège airports offer direct flights to various European cities, while Brussels Airport is just a short train ride away. Once in Wallonia, getting around is a breeze thanks to the excellent public transport system.

One of the best ways to explore Wallonia is on foot or by bike, as the region is home to some of the most beautiful hiking and cycling trails in Europe. Whether you're a seasoned athlete or a casual cyclist, Wallonia has something for everyone. From the gentle hills of the Ardennes to the picturesque countryside of Hainaut, there are countless trails to discover.

When it comes to food, Wallonia is famous for its hearty cuisine, with a focus on meat, cheese, and beer. Must-try dishes include carbonade flamande (beef stewed in beer), boulets à la liégeoise (meatballs in a sweet and sour sauce), and tarte au sucre (a delicious sugar pie). And of course, no trip to Wallonia would be complete without sampling some of the region's famous beers, including the Trappist beers of Chimay and Orval.

History buffs will love exploring Wallonia's many castles, fortresses, and museums. From the medieval Château de Bouillon to the World War II-era Fort de la Chartreuse, there is plenty to discover for those interested in the region's rich history. And for art lovers, the Musée des Beaux-Arts de Liège and the Musée Félicien Rops in Namur are not to be missed.

In conclusion, Wallonia is a fantastic destination for travelers looking to experience the best of Belgium. With its charming small towns, beautiful countryside, delicious food and drink, and rich cultural heritage, Wallonia has something for everyone. So come and explore this hidden gem of a region – you won't be disappointed!

Overview and history

Wallonia is the southern French-speaking region of Belgium and has a rich and fascinating history that is worth exploring. Here's an overview of Wallonia's history and what travelers can expect when visiting this region.

Overview:

Wallonia is one of the three regions of Belgium, along with Flanders and Brussels-Capital Region. It covers an area of about 16,844 square kilometers and has a population of approximately 3.6 million people. Wallonia is known for its picturesque cities, historic landmarks, and natural beauty, including the Ardennes Forest and the river Meuse.

History:

Wallonia's history dates to prehistoric times when it was inhabited by Celtic tribes. The region has been conquered and ruled by various groups over the centuries, including the Romans, Franks, and Burgundians. During the Middle Ages, Wallonia was an important center of trade and commerce and was home to several powerful feudal lords.

In the 16th century, Wallonia became part of the Spanish Netherlands and was ruled by Spain for several centuries. The region played a significant role in the Industrial Revolution, with the development of the coal and steel industries in the 19th and early 20th centuries. However, this period of prosperity was followed by a decline in the economy in the mid-20th century.

After World War II, Wallonia became a leading force in the European Union, with the creation of the European Coal and Steel Community in 1951. This led to a resurgence of the economy, and Wallonia became an important center of manufacturing, technology, and research.

Today, Wallonia is a thriving region with a diverse economy, rich culture, and stunning natural landscapes. It is home to several UNESCO World

Heritage sites, including the historic center of the city of Liège and the Belfries of Belgium and France.

Traveling in Wallonia:

When visiting Wallonia, travelers can expect to be greeted by friendly locals, delicious food, and a wealth of cultural and historical attractions. Some of the must-see destinations in Wallonia include:

Liège: This historic city is home to several museums, including the Grand Curtius Museum, which showcases the art and history of Liège, and the Museum of Walloon Life, which explores the region's culture and traditions.

Namur: The capital of Wallonia, Namur, is a charming city with a beautiful historic center, impressive fortifications, and stunning views of the river Meuse.

Dinant: This picturesque town is situated on the banks of the river Meuse and is known for its imposing Citadel, which offers stunning views of the town and the surrounding countryside.

Ardennes: The Ardennes Forest is a beautiful natural area that is perfect for hiking, cycling, and exploring. It is also home to several historic landmarks, including the Castle of Bouillon and the Fort of Huy.

Overall, Wallonia is a region with a rich and fascinating history, stunning natural landscapes, and a wealth of cultural and historical attractions. Whether you're interested in history, culture, or outdoor activities, Wallonia has something to offer everyone.

Welcome to Namur

Welcome to Namur, a charming city located in the Wallonia region of Belgium. Namur is the capital city of the Namur Province and is situated at the confluence of the Meuse and Sambre rivers, making it an ideal location for exploring the natural beauty of Belgium.

Namur is a city with a rich history and cultural heritage that dates to the Roman era.

Visitors can explore the Citadel of Namur, a UNESCO World Heritage site, which was built in the 13th century and played a significant role in the history of the region. The citadel offers stunning views of the city and surrounding countryside, and visitors can enjoy a guided tour to learn more about its history.

The city's historic center is home to a few beautiful buildings, including the St. Aubin's Cathedral, which dates back to the 18th century and features stunning Gothic architecture. The Place d'Armes is another popular destination in Namur, where visitors can enjoy the stunning architecture of the Hôtel de Ville (Town Hall) and the nearby Theatre Royal.

Namur is also famous for its vibrant arts and culture scene, with numerous galleries, museums, and exhibitions throughout the city. The Museum of Ancient Namur is a must-visit for history buffs, where visitors can learn about the city's Roman and Medieval past.

The Félicien Rops Museum is another popular destination, dedicated to the life and work of the renowned Belgian artist.

In addition to its cultural attractions, Namur is also known for its stunning natural beauty. Visitors can explore the Meuse and Sambre rivers by boat, or take a walk or bike ride along the banks. The Ardennes region, with its rolling hills and dense forests, is also a popular destination for outdoor enthusiasts.

Foodies will love the culinary delights on offer in Namur, with a variety of restaurants, cafes, and bars offering traditional Belgian dishes and international cuisine. Be sure to try some of the local specialties, such as moules-frites (mussels and fries) and carbonade flamande (beef stewed in beer).

If you're looking to experience the charm and beauty of Belgium, Namur is a destination not to be missed. With its rich history, vibrant culture scene, and stunning natural surroundings, there is something for everyone in this enchanting city.

5 must see attractions in Namur.

1. Citadel of Namur

The Citadel of Namur is a historic fortress located in the city of Namur, Belgium. Built in the 14th century, the citadel has played an important role in the region's military history, having been besieged and attacked many times over the centuries. Today, the Citadel of Namur is a popular tourist attraction, offering visitors a glimpse into the region's rich history.

Getting There:

The Citadel of Namur is in the heart of the city and is easily accessible by car, public transportation, or on foot. The closest train station is Namur Station, which is located about 1.5 kilometers from the citadel. From there, visitors can take a bus or taxi to reach the fortress. Additionally, there are several parking areas located near the citadel for those traveling by car.

Exploring the Citadel:

Visitors to the Citadel of Namur can take a guided tour to learn more about the fortress's history and the role it played in the region's military conflicts. The tours include visits to the underground tunnels and galleries, the former stables and barracks, and the gunpowder magazine. The citadel also offers several interactive exhibits, including a virtual reality experience that allows visitors to experience what it was like to be a soldier during a battle.

In addition to the historical exhibits, the Citadel of Namur also features several beautiful gardens and outdoor spaces, including the Jardin Félicien Rops, which offers stunning views of the city. Visitors can also take a stroll along the citadel's ramparts, which offer panoramic views of the Meuse River and the surrounding countryside.

Events and Activities:

Throughout the year, the Citadel of Namur hosts several events and activities for visitors of all ages. In the summer, the citadel is home to the Namur International Festival of Street Arts, which features performances by artists from around the world. The citadel also hosts a Christmas market during the holiday season, offering visitors the chance to shop for unique gifts and enjoy traditional Belgian foods and drinks.

Visiting Tips:

The Citadel of Namur is open year-round, but hours may vary depending on the season. It is recommended to check the citadel's website or call ahead to confirm hours of operation.

English, French, and Dutch are among the languages offered for the guided tours of the citadel.

Wear comfortable shoes as there are a lot of stairs and walking involved in exploring the citadel.

The citadel can be quite busy during peak tourist season, so it is recommended to arrive early in the day to avoid crowds.

Overall, the Citadel of Namur is a must-see attraction for visitors to Belgium, offering a fascinating glimpse into the region's rich history and military heritage.

2. St. Aubin's Cathedral

Saint Aubin's Cathedral is one of the most impressive and historically significant landmarks in Belgium. Located in the city of Namur, the cathedral is a popular tourist destination that attracts thousands of visitors each year. In this Belgium travel guidebook, we will explore the history of Saint Aubin's Cathedral, highlight some of its key features, and provide information on how to get there.

History of Saint Aubin's Cathedral

The origins of Saint Aubin's Cathedral can be traced back to the 10th century when a small chapel was built on the site. Over the years, the chapel was expanded and renovated several times until it was transformed into the impressive cathedral we see today.

Much of the cathedral's current architecture dates back to the 18th century when extensive renovations were carried out to enhance its grandeur.

Saint Aubin's Cathedral is dedicated to Saint Aubin, who was a bishop of Angers in the 6th century. Saint Aubin is also the patron saint of Namur, and his relics are enshrined in the cathedral.

The cathedral has played an important role in the religious and cultural history of the city of Namur, serving as a center for worship, education, and community gatherings.

Features of Saint Aubin's Cathedral

Saint Aubin's Cathedral is a stunning example of Baroque architecture, with its ornate façade, soaring bell towers, and intricately designed interior. The cathedral's interior features a collection of religious artwork and relics, including a 16th-century statue of Saint Aubin and a 17th-century altar. The cathedral's nave is lined with chapels, each dedicated to a different saint or religious figure.

One of the most striking features of Saint Aubin's Cathedral is its impressive organ. The cathedral's organ was built in the 18th century and is considered one of the most important organs in Belgium. The organ has undergone several renovations over the years, and today it is still used for concerts and special events.

Getting to Saint Aubin's Cathedral

Saint Aubin's Cathedral is in the heart of the city of Namur, making it easily accessible by public transportation or on foot. Visitors can take a train to the Namur train station, which is located just a short walk from the cathedral. Buses and taxis are also available for those who prefer not to walk.

For those who are driving, there are several parking options available near the cathedral.

There is several public parking lots within walking distance of the cathedral, as well as metered street parking.

Conclusion

Saint Aubin's Cathedral is a must-see attraction for anyone visiting Belgium, particularly those interested in religious and cultural history. The cathedral is a one-of-a-kind and unforgettable destination thanks to its beautiful architecture, rich history, and impressive features. With its central location in the city of Namur and easy accessibility, Saint Aubin's Cathedral is a perfect addition to any Belgium travel itinerary.

3. Félicien Rops Museum

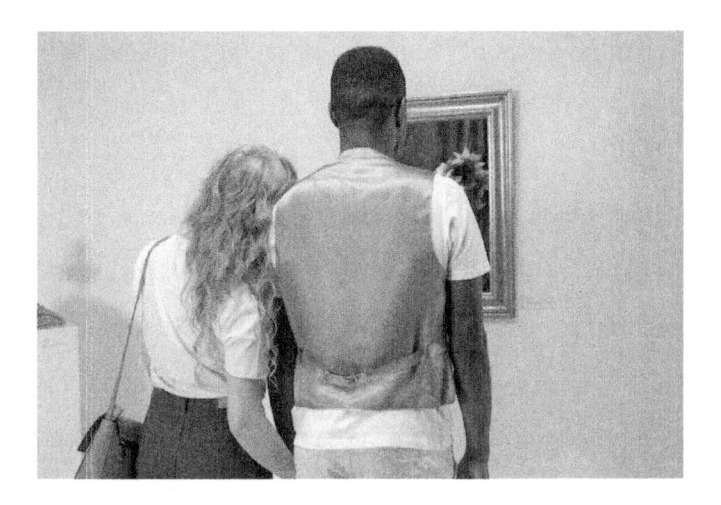

Félicien Rops Museum is a small but fascinating museum located in the heart of Namur, Belgium. Dedicated to the life and work of the Belgian artist Félicien Rops, the museum is a must-visit destination for art lovers, and anyone interested in Belgian culture.

Félicien Rops was a 19th-century Belgian artist known for his illustrations and prints, which often featured erotic and macabre themes. His work was controversial at the time, and he was frequently criticized for his provocative and daring subject matter. However, his work was also admired for its technical skill and artistic vision, and today he is considered one of the most important Belgian artists of the 19th century.

The Félicien Rops Museum houses a collection of his original artwork, including prints, drawings, and paintings. The museum also features a library with books and manuscripts related to Rops and his contemporaries. The museum is relatively small, but the collection is well-curated and provides a fascinating insight into Rops' life and artistic legacy.

Getting to the Félicien Rops Museum is easy, as it is in the heart of Namur, a city in the French-speaking region of Wallonia. Namur is easily accessible by train from Brussels, and the journey takes just over an hour. From the Namur train station, the museum is just a short walk away.

If you're driving, there are several parking garages located in the city center.

However, parking can be expensive and difficult to find during peak tourist season, so it's best to plan and arrive early.

Once you arrive at the museum, you'll be greeted by a small but inviting space that showcases Rops' artwork in a thoughtful and engaging way.

Every visitor to the museum is entitled to free admission from Tuesday through Sunday.

Overall, the Félicien Rops Museum is a must-visit destination for anyone traveling to Belgium, particularly for those interested in art and culture.

With its impressive collection of original artworks and its central location in Namur, it's the perfect place to immerse yourself in Belgian history and artistic legacy.

4. Namur Beer Festival

Namur Beer Festival is an annual event that takes place in the city of Namur, Belgium. The festival brings together beer lovers from all over the world to celebrate the rich history and culture of Belgian beer.

The festival takes place in the beautiful city of Namur, which is located in the heart of the Walloon Region of Belgium. The city is known for its stunning architecture, historic landmarks, and picturesque scenery. Visitors to the Namur Beer Festival will have the opportunity to explore the city's many attractions while also enjoying some of the best beer in the world.

The festival is typically held over the course of three days in late June or early July. During the festival, visitors can expect to find a wide variety of Belgian beers available for tasting. From classic Belgian styles like Dubbel, Tripel, and Saison to more modern craft beers, there is something for everyone at the Namur Beer Festival.

In addition to the beer tasting, the festival also features live music, food vendors, and beer-related activities. Visitors can participate in brewing workshops, learn about the history of Belgian beer, and even try their hand at beer pairing with local Belgian cuisine.

One of the highlights of the Namur Beer Festival is the opportunity to meet and mingle with some of the top brewers in Belgium. Visitors can chat with brewers, learn about their brewing techniques, and even purchase some of their beer to take home.

The festival is held in the historic Citadel of Namur, a massive fortress that has stood for centuries. The Citadel provides a stunning backdrop for the festival and adds to the overall atmosphere of the event.

For those looking to make the most of their trip to Namur, there are plenty of other attractions to explore in the city. Visitors can take a stroll along the picturesque banks of the Meuse River, visit the historic Belfry of Namur, or explore the city's many museums and art galleries.

Overall, the Namur Beer Festival is a must-visit event for any beer lover traveling to Belgium. With its wide variety of beers, lively atmosphere, and stunning location, it is a truly unforgettable experience that should not be missed.

4. Meuse River cruises

Meuse River Cruises: A Must-Do Experience in Belgium

Belgium is a country with a rich history and culture that has much to offer to visitors. One of the best ways to experience the beauty and charm of this country is by taking a river cruise on the Meuse River. The Meuse River is one of the major rivers in Europe, flowing through Belgium, France, and the Netherlands. In Belgium, the Meuse River flows through the beautiful countryside and past many historic towns and cities. A Meuse River cruise is a perfect way to explore this area and experience its beauty.

Why Take a Meuse River Cruise?

A Meuse River cruise is an unforgettable experience that allows you to see the beautiful landscapes and historic towns and cities of Belgium from a unique perspective.

As you glide along the river, you can admire the stunning scenery, from the lush green countryside to the medieval castles and charming villages that line the riverbanks.

A Meuse River cruise is also an opportunity to experience the local culture and cuisine of the region, as many cruises offer on-board dining and local excursions.

When to Take a Meuse River Cruise?

The best time to take a Meuse River cruise in Belgium is from April to October, as the weather is mild and pleasant during this time, and the river is navigable. The peak tourist season is from June to August, so it's advisable to book your cruise in advance to avoid disappointment.

What to Expect on a Meuse River Cruise?

A Meuse River cruise typically lasts between one and two hours, although longer cruises are available. The boats used for the cruises vary in size and style, from modern and luxurious to more traditional and rustic. On-board facilities often include dining areas, bars, and panoramic windows for stunning views of the passing scenery. Some cruises also offer guided tours of the local attractions, such as the medieval town of Dinant, the citadel of Namur, or the historic city of Liege.

Popular Meuse River Cruise Routes

There are several popular routes for Meuse River cruises in Belgium, each offering a unique experience of the region. Among the most well-liked routes are:

Dinant to Anseremme: This route takes you past the scenic cliffs of the Meuse Valley and the charming town of Anseremme, with its historic church and castle.

Namur to Huy: This route takes you past the impressive citadel of Namur and the historic town of

Huy, with its medieval castle and ancient Roman ruins.

Liege to Maastricht: This route takes you past the historic city of Liege, with its stunning cathedral and charming old town, and on to the Dutch city of Maastricht, known for its rich history and vibrant culture.

Tips for Taking a Meuse River Cruise

Here are some tips to make the most of your Meuse River cruise experience:

Dress appropriately for the weather, and wear comfortable shoes, as you may need to walk to and from the boat.

Bring a camera to capture the stunning views of the passing scenery.

Book your cruise in advance to avoid disappointment, especially during peak season.

Check the itinerary of your cruise to see what sights and attractions are included, and plan accordingly.

Conclusion

A Meuse River cruise is a must-do experience for anyone visiting Belgium. It's an opportunity to explore the beauty and charm of this country from a unique perspective, while also experiencing its rich culture and cuisine. Whether you're interested in history, architecture, or simply enjoying the natural beauty of the region, a Meuse River cruise is an unforgettable experience that you won't want to miss.

Welcome to Liège

Welcome to Liège, a beautiful city located in the French-speaking region of Wallonia in Belgium. Known for its rich history, stunning architecture, and vibrant cultural scene, Liège is a must-visit destination for any traveler exploring Belgium.

Getting to Liège is easy, with the city accessible by train from most major cities in Belgium and France. The nearest airport is Brussels Airport, located approximately one hour away by car or train.

Once you arrive in Liège, there are plenty of things to see and do. The city is home to a number of historic landmarks, including the prince-Bishops' Palace, which dates back to the 16th century and is now home to the Provincial Government of Liège. The Palace of the Prince-Bishops is also worth a visit, as it offers stunning views of the city and its surroundings.

Another must-see attraction in Liège is the Cathedral of St. Paul, a beautiful example of Gothic architecture that has stood in the heart of the city since the 10th century. The cathedral features stunning stained-glass windows and intricate carvings, making it a popular destination for art lovers and history buffs alike.

For those interested in learning more about Liège's rich history, a visit to the Grand Curtius Museum is a must. Housed in a beautiful 17th-century building, the museum features a wide range of exhibits showcasing the city's cultural heritage, from ancient artifacts to contemporary art.

For foodies, Liège is also a paradise. The city is known for its delicious waffles, made with a special dough recipe that includes chunks of sugar, giving them a crunchy texture and unique flavor. Other culinary highlights of Liège include the local specialty, boulets à la liégeoise, a meatball dish served with a savory sauce made from onions and beer.

Finally, if you're looking for a lively cultural scene, Liège won't disappoint. The city is home to a number of theaters, music venues, and galleries, showcasing the work of both local and international artists. Be sure to check out the annual Liège International Jazz Festival, held every year in July, which attracts top musicians from around the world.

5 must see attractions in Liege.

1. Liège-Guillemins railway station

Liège-Guillemins railway station is a stunning example of modern architecture and one of the most impressive railway stations in Europe. Located in Liège, Belgium, it is the main railway station in the city and an important hub for train travel throughout Belgium and beyond.

Designed by the Spanish architect Santiago Calatrava, the station was opened in 2009 and is an impressive work of art. It is characterized by its steel and glass roof, which spans the entire length of the station and creates a spacious, light-filled interior. The roof is supported by 600 steel columns, and the station is designed to accommodate up to 36,000 passengers per day.

The Liège-Guillemins railway station has won several awards for its design, including the 2010 European Union Prize for Contemporary Architecture, and it is one of the most important modern architectural landmarks in Belgium.

The station offers a wide range of services and amenities, including restaurants, cafes, shops, and a tourist information center. There is also a car park, a bicycle parking area, and easy access for disabled passengers.

The station is served by both high-speed trains and local trains, with connections to major Belgian cities such as Brussels, Antwerp, and Bruges, as well as international destinations such as Paris, Amsterdam, and Cologne. The high-speed trains that serve the station are known as the Thalys, which operate between Paris, Brussels, Amsterdam, and Cologne.

One of the most impressive features of the station is the central hall, which is flooded with natural light and offers a stunning view of the roof. The hall is also home to a large digital clock, which displays the time and train information for passengers.

For visitors to Liège, the station is a must-see attraction. The building is easily accessible by public transport, and visitors can take a guided tour to learn more about the station's history and design. There are also many hotels and restaurants located nearby, making it a convenient base for exploring the city.

2. Prince-Bishops' Palace

The prince-Bishops' Palace, also known as the Palais des Princes-Evêques in French, is a stunning palace located in the heart of the historic city center of Liège, Belgium. This impressive building served as the residence of the prince-Bishops of Liège for over 800 years, from the 11th century to the French Revolution. Today, it stands as a testament to the city's rich history and cultural heritage and is a must-see attraction for anyone visiting Liège.

The Palace was originally built as a fortress in the 10th century and was expanded over the centuries to become a grand palace. The palace's architecture is a beautiful blend of Gothic and Renaissance styles, with intricate stonework, vaulted ceilings, and ornate carvings. Visitors to the palace can explore the grand reception rooms, the impressive courtyard, and the beautiful gardens, which offer stunning views of the city.

The Palace is now home to several museums, including the Museum of Walloon Art, which houses a collection of art from the region, and the Museum of Religious Art and Mosan Art, which showcases the religious art of the Mosan Valley.

The palace also features a museum dedicated to the history of Liège, with exhibits on the city's history, industry, and cultural heritage.

One of the most popular attractions of the Palace is the Gothic Room, which features stunning frescoes and an ornate fireplace. This room was once used for important ceremonies and gatherings and offers a glimpse into the opulence and grandeur of the prince-Bishops' court.

The palace is also home to the Archaeological Museum of Liège, which showcases the city's rich archaeological heritage. Visitors can see a wide range of artifacts from the Roman and medieval periods, including tools, pottery, jewelry, and weapons.

The palace's gardens are a lovely oasis in the middle of the city, providing a tranquil respite from the commotion. The gardens feature fountains, sculptures, and beautifully manicured lawns, making them a popular spot for picnics and leisurely walks.

The Palace is located in the heart of Liège, making it easily accessible to visitors. It is open to the public year-round, with varying opening hours depending on the season. Guided tours are available, offering visitors an in-depth look at the palace's history and architecture.

In conclusion, the prince-Bishops' Palace is a magnificent palace that offers a glimpse into Liège's rich history and cultural heritage. With its stunning architecture, beautiful gardens, and fascinating museums, it is a must-see attraction for anyone visiting Liège.

2. St. Paul's Cathedral

St. Paul's Cathedral in Liège, Belgium, is one of the city's most famous landmarks and a must-visit destination for travelers interested in history, architecture, and religion. This impressive cathedral has a rich history dating back to the 10th century and boasts a striking Gothic-style façade that is sure to impress visitors.

History of St. Paul's Cathedral

St. Paul's Cathedral was originally built in the 10th century on the site of a Romanesque church that had been destroyed. The original building was dedicated to Saint Paul the Apostle and served as the cathedral of Liège until the 18th century when it was destroyed by fire. The current cathedral was built in the 19th century, following the plans of architect Louis Roelandt.

Architecture of St. Paul's Cathedral

The current St. Paul's Cathedral is a beautiful example of Gothic Revival architecture. The façade of the cathedral is adorned with intricate carvings and features two towers that rise up to a height of 64 meters. The interior of the cathedral is just as impressive, with vaulted ceilings, stained glass windows, and beautiful sculptures.

One of the most impressive features of the cathedral is the organ, which dates back to the 18th century. The organ has been restored several times over the years and is now one of the largest and most beautiful organs in Belgium. Visitors can attend concerts and other musical performances in the cathedral, which are a wonderful way to experience the building's acoustics.

Visiting St. Paul's Cathedral

St. Paul's Cathedral is in the heart of Liège and is easily accessible by public transportation. The cathedral is open to visitors throughout the year, with hours varying depending on the season. Admission to the cathedral is free, although donations are appreciated.

Visitors should plan to spend at least an hour exploring the cathedral and its many features. Guided tours are available, although visitors can also explore on their own. The cathedral is wheelchair accessible and has a gift shop where visitors can purchase souvenirs and other items.

Conclusion

St. Paul's Cathedral in Liège is a must-visit destination for travelers to Belgium. With its rich history, stunning architecture, and beautiful music, the cathedral is a true gem of the city. Whether you're interested in religion, architecture, or history, St. Paul's Cathedral is sure to delight and inspire you.

3. La Batte market

La Batte Market is one of the largest and oldest markets in Belgium, located in the city of Liège. This bustling market has been held every Sunday morning for over 450 years, making it a must-visit destination for anyone traveling to Belgium.

History and Background:

La Batte Market dates back to the 14th century when it was established as a livestock market. Over the centuries, it evolved into a general market where vendors sold a variety of goods such as food, clothing, and household items. Today, the market spans several streets and attracts thousands of visitors each week.

What to Expect:

Visitors to La Batte Market can expect a vibrant and lively atmosphere filled with vendors shouting out prices and bargaining with customers. The market offers a wide range of products, from fresh produce to antiques, second-hand clothes to handmade crafts, and much more.

Food:

One of the highlights of La Batte Market is the incredible selection of fresh food available. Vendors sell everything from seasonal fruits and vegetables to fresh meats, cheeses, and bread. Visitors can also sample local specialties such as Liège waffles, boulets Lieges (meatballs in a Liège sauce), and tarte au riz (rice pudding tart).

Antiques:

For those interested in antiques, La Batte Market has a large selection of vendors selling vintage and antique items. Visitors can find everything from antique furniture to vintage clothing and jewelry, as well as more unusual items such as old books and records.

Artisan Crafts:

Visitors to La Batte Market can also discover a variety of handmade crafts, including pottery, textiles, and woodworking. Many of the craftspeople at the market are local artists, providing a unique insight into the traditional crafts of the region.

Shopping Tips:

To make the most of your visit to La Batte Market, arrive early in the morning to avoid the crowds and take advantage of the best deals. Don't be afraid to bargain with vendors but be respectful and polite. Having cash on hand is also a good idea because not all vendors accept credit cards.

Location and Hours:

La Batte Market is in the heart of Liège, along the banks of the Meuse River. The market takes place every Sunday morning from 8:00 am to 2:30 pm, rain or shine.

In conclusion, La Batte Market is a unique and exciting experience for anyone traveling to Belgium. With its rich history and diverse selection of goods, the market provides a glimpse into the local culture and is not to be missed.

5. Les Ardentes music festival

Les Ardentes Music Festival is one of the most popular and exciting music festivals in Belgium. It takes place every year in early July and attracts thousands of music lovers from around the country and beyond. If you're planning a trip to Belgium and want to experience some of the best live music around, then Les Ardentes is a must-visit event.

History of Les Ardentes Music Festival

Les Ardentes Music Festival was first launched in 2006, and it has since become one of the most anticipated music events in Belgium. The festival takes place in the beautiful Parc Astrid, which is in the city of Liège. It started as a small-scale event, but it has grown over the years to become a major fixture on the Belgian music scene.

Music and Lineup

One of the reasons that Les Ardentes Music Festival has become so popular is because of the diverse lineup of artists that it attracts. The festival features a mix of both international and Belgian acts, spanning a variety of genres, from pop and rock to hip-hop and electronic music.

Some of the big names that have graced the stages at Les Ardentes include The Black Keys, Travis Scott, Kendrick Lamar, and Muse, among others. The festival also offers opportunities for up-and-coming artists to showcase their talents, so there is always a mix of established and emerging talent on the lineup.

Aside from the main stages, Les Ardentes also features a variety of smaller stages and areas where DJs and other artists perform. This adds to the overall festival experience, providing a diverse range of musical styles to enjoy.

Location and Accessibility

As previously mentioned, Les Ardentes takes place in Parc Astrid, which is in Liège. The park is conveniently located near the city center, making it easily accessible by public transportation, bike, or on foot.

The park itself is a beautiful setting for the festival, with plenty of green spaces and areas to relax between performances. There are also a variety of food and drink options available on-site, so you can stay fueled up and ready to enjoy the music all day and night.

Tips for Attending Les Ardentes Music Festival

If you're planning to attend Les Ardentes Music Festival, there are a few things to keep in mind to make the most of your experience. Here are some pointers to aid your preparation:

Buy tickets in advance: Les Ardentes Music Festival tends to sell out quickly, so it's best to buy your tickets well in advance to avoid disappointment.

Bring appropriate clothing: The festival takes place in early July, which can be quite warm in Belgium.

Be sure to bring clothing that is comfortable and appropriate for the weather, as well as sunscreen and a hat to protect yourself from the sun.

Plan your schedule: With so many artists performing, it's important to plan out your schedule in advance to make sure you don't miss any of your favorite acts.

Be prepared for crowds: Les Ardentes attracts a large crowd, so be prepared for long lines, crowded stages, and busy food and drink areas.

Take breaks: With so much music and activity going on, it's important to take breaks and rest your feet and ears. There are plenty of places to sit and relax in Parc Astrid, so take advantage of them when you need a break.

In conclusion, Les Ardentes Music Festival is a must-visit event for music lovers visiting Belgium. With its diverse lineup of artists, beautiful setting, and lively atmosphere, it's an experience that you won't forget. Be sure to plan, bring appropriate clothing, and take breaks when needed to make the most of your festival experience.

Welcome to Dinant

Welcome to Dinant, a charming town located in the province of Namur in the Wallonia region of Belgium. Dinant is situated on the banks of the river Meuse and is known for its stunning scenery, rich history, and vibrant cultural scene.

Dinant is a popular destination for tourists and travelers, and there are plenty of things to see and do here. Whether you're interested in exploring the town's historical landmarks, enjoying outdoor activities, or indulging in the local cuisine and drinks, Dinant has something for everyone.

Historical Landmarks:

One of the most iconic landmarks in Dinant is the Collegiate Church of Our Lady, a stunning Gothic-style church that dates back to the 13th century. The church features intricate stained-glass windows and impressive stone carvings, and it offers breathtaking views of the town and the river from its hilltop location.

Another must-see attraction in Dinant is the Citadel of Dinant, a fortress perched high on a rocky outcrop overlooking the town. The citadel dates to the 11th century and has served various purposes throughout history, from defending the town to serving as a prison. Today, it houses a museum that showcases the history of the fortress and the town.

Outdoor Activities:

Dinant is surrounded by stunning natural landscapes, making it an excellent destination for outdoor activities such as hiking, biking, and kayaking. The town is situated on the Meuse River, which offers plenty of opportunities for water sports and leisurely boat rides. Additionally, the nearby Ardennes Forest is home to several hiking trails and cycling routes, including the famous La Veloroute de la Meuse, a 160 km bike path that runs from Dinant to Maastricht in the Netherlands.

Local Cuisine and Drinks:

Belgium is famous for its culinary scene, and Dinant is no exception. The town is renowned for its delicious regional specialties, such as couque de Dinant, a hard and crunchy gingerbread-like biscuit made with honey, and escavèche, a type of fish served in a marinade of vinegar, oil, and spices. Dinant is also home to several breweries and distilleries, where you can sample local beers and spirits such as Leffe, Chimay, and Peket.

In conclusion, Dinant is a beautiful and captivating town that offers a perfect mix of history, nature, and culture.

Whether you're interested in exploring the town's historical landmarks, enjoying outdoor activities, or indulging in the local cuisine and drinks, Dinant is sure to delight and inspire you. So, pack your bags and get ready for a wonderful adventure in this charming town!

5 must see attractions in Dinant.

1. Citadel of Dinant

The Citadel of Dinant is one of the most impressive historical landmarks in Belgium. Perched high on a rocky outcrop overlooking the town of Dinant and the River Meuse, the fortress is a must-see attraction for anyone interested in history, architecture, and military heritage. Here is everything you need to know about the Citadel of Dinant for your Belgium travel guidebook.

History:

The Citadel of Dinant has a rich and fascinating history that spans more than a thousand years. The fortress was first built in the 11th century to defend the town from invading forces. Over the centuries, it has been expanded and modified several times, serving various purposes throughout its history, from military fortress to state prison.

During World War I, the Citadel of Dinant was used as a strategic defense point by the Belgian army. In August 1914, it was attacked and occupied by German forces, who used it as a base for their subsequent invasion of Belgium. In 1940, during World War II, the fortress was again used as a defense point, this time by the French army.

Today, the Citadel of Dinant is a popular tourist attraction and museum that showcases the history of the fortress and the town. Visitors can explore the various parts of the fortress, including the underground tunnels, the ramparts, and the top of the rocky outcrop, which offers stunning panoramic views of the town and the river.

Architecture:

The Citadel of Dinant is a stunning example of military architecture, with its complex system of walls, towers, and fortifications. The fortress is built on a rocky outcrop that rises 100 meters above the

River Meuse, providing a natural defense against enemy attacks. Its walls are made of limestone and were designed to withstand cannon fire and other types of artillery.

The Citadel also features several architectural elements that reflect its various uses throughout history. For example, the 17th-century Gothic-style church of Saint-Martin was built inside the fortress to serve the religious needs of the soldiers and prisoners. The fortress also has a 19th-century barracks and a 20th-century military hospital.

Museum:

The Citadel of Dinant houses a museum that showcases the history of the fortress and the town. The museum features a wide range of exhibits, including weapons, uniforms, and equipment used by soldiers throughout history. Visitors can also explore the various parts of the fortress and learn about the daily life of soldiers and prisoners who lived here.

The museum also has a special exhibit dedicated to the famous saxophonist Adolphe Sax, who was born in Dinant in 1814. Sax invented the saxophone and other musical instruments and is considered one of the most important figures in the history of modern music.

In conclusion, the Citadel of Dinant is a must-see attraction for anyone interested in history, architecture, and military heritage. Its rich and fascinating history, stunning architecture, and breathtaking views make it a highlight of any visit to Belgium.

So, make sure to add it to your travel itinerary and immerse yourself in the fascinating world of the Citadel of Dinant.

2. Adolphe Sax House

The Adolphe Sax House is a historic museum located in the city of Dinant in Belgium. It is named after Adolphe Sax, a famous Belgian musician and inventor who is best known for inventing the saxophone.

History of the Adolphe Sax House

The Adolphe Sax House was originally built in the 18th century as a residence for the mayor of Dinant. In the early 19th century, it was purchased by Adolphe Sax's father, Charles-Joseph Sax, who was a prominent instrument maker in the city. Adolphe Sax was born in this house on November 6, 1814, and spent his early years learning the trade of instrument making from his father.

After Adolphe Sax left Dinant to pursue his career as a musician and inventor, the house was sold to various owners and fell into disrepair. In the 1970s, the city of Dinant purchased the property and began a restoration project to turn it into a museum dedicated to Adolphe Sax.

What to see at the Adolphe Sax House

Today, the Adolphe Sax House is a fascinating museum that tells the story of Adolphe Sax's life and work. Visitors can explore the house where Sax was born and see a collection of his original instruments, including saxophones, clarinets, and horns. The museum also features interactive exhibits that allow visitors to learn about the physics of sound and the history of music.

One of the highlights of the museum is the opportunity to play a saxophone. Visitors of all ages can try their hand at playing this iconic instrument and feel the same thrill that Adolphe Sax must have felt when he first invented it.

In addition to the museum exhibits, the Adolphe Sax House also hosts concerts and other musical events throughout the year. These events showcase the talents of local musicians and pay tribute to the legacy of Adolphe Sax.

Tips for visiting the Adolphe Sax House

The Adolphe Sax House is open to visitors year-round, with varying hours depending on the season. Admission fees are reasonable, and discounts are available for children, students, and seniors.

To make the most of your visit, consider taking a guided tour of the museum. These tours are led by knowledgeable guides who can provide insights into Adolphe Sax's life and work.

After your visit to the Adolphe Sax House, be sure to take some time to explore the city of Dinant. This charming town is home to several other historic buildings, as well as a scenic riverside promenade and a picturesque citadel.

3. Collegiate Church of Notre-Dame

The Collegiate Church of Notre-Dame is one of the most beautiful and historically significant landmarks in Belgium. Located in the heart of the city of Dinant, this stunning Gothic church is renowned for its impressive architecture, rich history, and unique artistic treasures.

History of the Collegiate Church of Notre-Dame
of Notre-Dame dates to
The Collegiate Church the 13th century when it was founded by the Bishop of Liège, Albert de Cuyck. Over the centuries, the church underwent several renovations and restorations, with the most

significant work being carried out in the 16th and 17th centuries.

During the French Revolution, the Collegiate Church of Notre-Dame suffered extensive damage, and many of its priceless works of art were destroyed. It wasn't until the mid-19th century that the church was restored to its former glory, thanks to the efforts of several prominent architects and art historians.

Architecture of the Collegiate Church of Notre-Dame

The Collegiate Church of Notre-Dame is a masterpiece of Gothic architecture, characterized by its soaring vaulted ceilings, intricate stone carvings, and stunning stained-glass windows. The church's façade is particularly impressive, featuring a series of intricate spires and a magnificent rose window that is considered one of the finest examples of Gothic art in Belgium.

Inside the church, visitors will be struck by the beauty of the nave, which is lined with ornate stone pillars and arches. The choir is also a highlight, with its stunning Gothic vaulted ceiling and richly decorated altarpiece.

Artistic Treasures of the Collegiate Church of Notre-Dame

The Collegiate Church of Notre-Dame is home to an impressive collection of artistic treasures, including several notable works by renowned Flemish artists. Among the highlights are:

The pulpit, which was sculpted by the famous 18th-century artist Laurent Delvaux. The pulpit features intricate carvings of biblical scenes and figures, including Moses, Elijah, and John the Baptist.

The altarpiece, which was created by the Flemish painter and sculptor Jean-Baptiste Capronnier in the 19th century. The altarpiece depicts scenes from the life of Christ and is considered one of the most important works of religious art in Belgium.

The stained-glass windows, which are among the finest examples of Gothic art in Belgium. The windows feature intricate designs and vivid colors, depicting scenes from the Bible and the lives of the saints.

Visiting the Collegiate Church of Notre-Dame

The Collegiate Church of Notre-Dame is open to visitors year-round, and admission is free. Guided tours are available for those who wish to learn more about the church's history and architecture, and audio guides are also available in several languages.

In addition to its religious significance and artistic treasures, the Collegiate Church of Notre-Dame is also a popular destination for music lovers. The church hosts regular concerts throughout the year, featuring performances by some of the world's most talented musicians.

Overall, the Collegiate Church of Notre-Dame is a must-visit destination for anyone traveling to Belgium. With its stunning architecture, rich history, and unique artistic treasures, this beautiful Gothic church is sure to leave a lasting impression on all who visit.

4. Les Saxophones du Monde

Les Saxophones du Monde is a unique and fascinating attraction located in Dinant, Belgium. As the birthplace of Adolphe Sax, the inventor of the saxophone, Dinant is a natural location for a museum dedicated to this iconic musical instrument.

Les Saxophones du Monde, which translates to "The Saxophones of the World," is a museum and performance venue that celebrates the saxophone's rich history and enduring appeal.

The museum's collection includes over 500 saxophones from around the world, dating back to the instrument's invention in the 1840s. Visitors can see and hear examples of different types of saxophones, including soprano, alto, tenor, and baritone saxophones, as well as rarer instruments like the bass and contrabass saxophones. The collection includes saxophones made from a variety of materials, including brass, silver, and even wood.

In addition to the extensive collection of saxophones, Les Saxophones du Monde also features interactive exhibits that allow visitors to learn more about the instrument's history and how it works. Visitors can listen to audio recordings of saxophone music from around the world and watch videos that demonstrate different playing techniques.

One of the highlights of a visit to Les Saxophones du Monde is the opportunity to attend a live performance. The museum regularly hosts concerts featuring local and international saxophonists, as well as jazz and classical music ensembles. The acoustics of the museum's performance hall are exceptional, making it an ideal venue for enjoying the rich, warm tones of the saxophone.

Les Saxophones du Monde is in the heart of Dinant, a picturesque town on the banks of the Meuse River. Dinant is known for its stunning citadel, which overlooks the town and offers panoramic views of the surrounding countryside. The town is also famous for its delicious cuisine, including locally produced cheeses, chocolates, and beers.

Visitors to Dinant can easily spend a day exploring the town and its many attractions, including the

Gothic-style Collegiate Church of Notre-Dame, the charming Maison de Monsieur Sax (the former home of Adolphe Sax), and the beautiful Leffe Abbey. Outdoor enthusiasts will enjoy hiking or biking along the river, while history buffs can explore the town's rich medieval heritage.

Whether you're a music lover, a history buff, or simply looking for a unique and memorable experience, Les Saxophones du Monde is a must-see attraction in Belgium. With its extensive collection of saxophones, interactive exhibits, and live performances, this museum offers a fascinating glimpse into the history and enduring appeal of one of the world's most beloved musical instruments.

5. Dinant Jazz Nights

Dinant Jazz Nights: A Must-See for Music Lovers in Belgium

Dinant Jazz Nights is an annual music festival that takes place in the charming town of Dinant, Belgium. The festival has become a highlight of the Belgian jazz scene, attracting both local and international musicians, as well as jazz enthusiasts from all over the world.

History of Dinant Jazz Nights

The first edition of Dinant Jazz Nights took place in 1983, organized by a group of passionate music lovers. Over the years, the festival has grown in popularity, and today it is one of the most important jazz events in Belgium. The festival has a rich history, with some of the biggest names in jazz having performed there, including Chet Baker, Toots Thielemans, and Dizzy Gillespie, to name just a few.

What to Expect at Dinant Jazz Nights

Dinant Jazz Nights is a four-day festival that takes place in late July or early August. The festival attracts both established jazz musicians and up-and-coming talents, offering a diverse program that includes both classical and contemporary jazz, as well as other related genres such as blues and soul.

The festival takes place in a variety of venues throughout the town of Dinant, including the Collegiate Church of Notre-Dame, Bayard Rock, and the Charles Deliège Hall. The venues are all within walking distance of each other, making it easy to move between them and catch as many performances as possible.

In addition to the concerts, the festival also features workshops and masterclasses, giving visitors the opportunity to learn from some of the best jazz musicians in the world. The festival also has a vibrant atmosphere, with food and drink stalls lining the streets, and a general sense of celebration and excitement.

How to Get to Dinant Jazz Nights

Dinant is in the French-speaking region of Wallonia in Belgium, about an hour and a half drive from Brussels. Visitors can also take the train to Dinant from Brussels or other major Belgian cities.

Once in Dinant, visitors can easily walk between the festival venues, or take a local bus or taxi if they prefer.

Tips for Visiting Dinant Jazz Nights

Book your tickets early: Dinant Jazz Nights is a popular festival, and tickets can sell out quickly. It's best to book your tickets as early as possible to avoid disappointment.

Dress for the weather: The festival takes place in the summer, so make sure to dress accordingly. Bring a light jacket or sweater for cooler evenings.

Stay in Dinant: To fully immerse yourself in the festival, consider staying in Dinant for a few nights. There are plenty of accommodation options available, from budget-friendly hostels to luxurious hotels.

Explore the town: Dinant is a picturesque town with plenty of attractions to explore. Take some time to wander the streets, visit the Citadel of Dinant, and sample some of the local cuisine.

In Conclusion

Dinant Jazz Nights is a must-see for anyone who loves jazz music. With its diverse program, vibrant atmosphere, and charming setting, it's easy to see why this festival has become such an important event in the Belgian jazz scene. Whether you're a seasoned jazz aficionado or simply curious about the genre, Dinant Jazz Nights is an experience you won't forget.

Accommodations in Wallonia

Wallonia is the French-speaking region of Belgium, known for its scenic beauty, rich cultural heritage, and delicious cuisine. With a variety of accommodations ranging from budget-friendly options to luxurious resorts, Wallonia is a great destination for all kinds of travelers.

Hotels

Wallonia has a wide selection of hotels to choose from, ranging from budget-friendly options to luxury hotels. In cities such as Brussels, Namur, and Liege, you'll find a variety of international hotel chains, as well as locally owned boutique hotels. The hotel rates in Wallonia vary depending on the season and location, but they are generally cheaper than those in Brussels.

Bed and Breakfasts

Bed and breakfasts are a great option for travelers who want to experience the local culture and hospitality. Wallonia has many charming bed and breakfasts that offer a cozy and intimate atmosphere. You'll find them in both rural and urban areas, and they often provide a hearty breakfast made with locally sourced ingredients.

Guesthouses

Guesthouses are like bed and breakfasts, but they typically offer more amenities such as a restaurant, bar, or spa. They are often located in historic buildings and provide a unique and authentic experience. You can find guesthouses in both urban and rural areas of Wallonia.

Holiday Cottages

Holiday cottages, also known as gites, are self-catering accommodations that offer a home away from home experience. They are perfect for families or groups of friends who want to enjoy a private and comfortable space. In Wallonia, you'll find holiday cottages in both rural and urban areas, and they range from small cottages to large farmhouses.

Campgrounds

If you're an outdoor enthusiast, Wallonia has plenty of campgrounds that offer a chance to experience the region's natural beauty. You can choose from basic campsites with just a patch of grass and a fire pit to full-service campsites that offer amenities such as electricity, showers, and Wi-Fi. Camping in Wallonia is a great way to connect with nature and save money on accommodation.

Luxury Resorts

For those seeking a luxurious and indulgent experience, Wallonia has a variety of high-end resorts that offer world-class amenities such as spas, fine dining, and golf courses. Many of these resorts are in scenic areas such as the Ardennes and offer stunning views of the surrounding landscape. These resorts are perfect for romantic getaways or special occasions.

In conclusion, Wallonia offers a variety of accommodations for all kinds of travelers. Whether you're looking for a budget-friendly option or a luxurious retreat, you're sure to find something that suits your needs. With its rich history, beautiful scenery, and delicious cuisine, Wallonia is a destination that should not be missed on your trip to Belgium.

15 must try Food and drink in Wallonia.

Wallonia, the southern French-speaking region of Belgium, is a food lover's paradise. From hearty stews to delicate pastries, there is a rich culinary heritage that is unique to this region. Here are 15 must-try foods and drinks in Wallonia:

Carbonnade flamande: This beef and beef stew is a classic dish from Wallonia. The beef is cooked in beer, onions, and spices until it is melt-in-your-mouth tender.

Liège waffles: These are not your average waffles. Liège waffles are made with a brioche-like dough and have pearl sugar that caramelizes when cooked.

Ardennes ham: This cured ham from the Ardennes region is a must-try. It has a distinct smoky flavor and is delicious served with bread and cheese.

Waterzooi: This creamy stew is made with chicken or fish and vegetables. It's thickened with cream and egg yolks and is perfect for a cold day.

Boulets à la liégeoise: These are meatballs made with a mix of pork and beef and are served with a sweet and sour sauce made with beer, onions, and apple syrup.

Rochefort Trappist beer: This beer is brewed by Trappist monks and is only one of six beers in the world to have the Trappist label.

Tarte au riz: This rice tart is a traditional dessert from the Hainaut region. It's made with rice pudding, short crust pastry, and dusted with powdered sugar.

Poteen liégeoise: This is a hearty stew made with pork, potatoes, cabbage, and carrots. It's perfect for a cold winter day.

Escavèche: This is a traditional fish dish that is marinated in vinegar and served cold. It's typically served with bread or potatoes.

Jambon d'Ardenne: This is another type of cured ham from the Ardennes region. It's typically served with bread and cheese.

Elixir d'Anvers: This is a liqueur made with a secret recipe of herbs and spices. It has a sweet and spicy flavor and is often served as an after-dinner drink.

Salade liégeoise: This is a salad made with green beans, potatoes, bacon, and a vinaigrette dressing. It's a great side dish for any meal.

Pain à la grecque: This sweet bread is made with honey, almonds, and orange blossom water. It's perfect for breakfast or as a dessert.

Orval Trappist beer: This beer is brewed by Trappist monks and is known for its complex flavors of fruit, spice, and hops.

Frites: Belgium is known for its frites, and Wallonia is no exception. These thick-cut fries are typically served with mayonnaise or a variety of sauces.

Whether you're a foodie or just looking to try something new, Wallonia has plenty of delicious dishes and drinks to explore. Be sure to add these 15 must-try foods and drinks to your list when planning your trip to this region of Belgium.

Events and festivals in Wallonia

Wallonia, the French-speaking southern region of Belgium, is a culturally rich and diverse area that is home to a variety of festivals and events throughout the year. From music and dance to food and folklore, there is something for everyone in Wallonia. Here are some of the most popular events and festivals that you won't want to miss when visiting this vibrant region:

Durbuy Christmas Market - Held in the picturesque town of Durbuy, this Christmas market is one of the most beautiful in Wallonia. Visitors can enjoy festive music, holiday treats, and browse the many stalls selling artisanal gifts and crafts. The market takes place from late November to early January.

Fêtes de Wallonie - Celebrated in September, this festival is a celebration of Walloon culture and tradition. Visitors can enjoy traditional music, dance, and food, and participate in various activities such as parades and folk games. The festival takes place in various cities throughout Wallonia.

Les Ardentes - Held in the city of Liège in July, Les Ardentes is a popular music festival that attracts a diverse lineup of artists from around the world. Visitors can enjoy a variety of genres including rock, hip hop, and electronic music.

Binche Carnival - This traditional carnival is held in the town of Binche in February and is recognized as a UNESCO Intangible Cultural Heritage. Visitors can witness the famous Gilles, who wear elaborate costumes and masks and throw oranges to the crowds. The carnival also features parades, music, and food.

Spa Francorchamps F1 Grand Prix - Held annually in August, this world-renowned motor racing event takes place on the iconic Spa Francorchamps circuit. Visitors can witness some of the fastest cars and best drivers in the world competing on one of the most challenging tracks in motorsports.

Namur en Mai - This festival is held in the city of Namur in May and features music, dance, and theater performances from around the world. Visitors can enjoy free outdoor concerts, street performances, and food stalls offering local specialties.

Mons International Love Film Festival - This film festival is held in the city of Mons in February and features a selection of international films focused on love and relationships. Visitors can attend screenings, meet with directors and actors, and participate in discussions and workshops.

Wallonia Festival - Held in the city of Louvain-la-Neuve in October, this festival is a celebration of Wallonia's cultural diversity. Visitors can enjoy a variety of music, dance, and theater performances, as well as workshops and activities focused on the region's heritage.

Les Nuits de Septembre - This music festival is held in the city of Liège in September and features a variety of genres, including rock, jazz, and classical music. Visitors can enjoy outdoor concerts and events, as well as indoor performances in venues throughout the city.

Tournai International Tapestry Biennial - Held every two years in the city of Tournai, this biennial celebrates the art of tapestry-making with exhibitions featuring works from around the world. Visitors can also participate in workshops and activities focused on this unique craft.

In addition to these events and festivals, Wallonia is home to a variety of food and drink festivals, including the Brussels Beer Festival in September and the Huy Chocolate Festival in December. No matter what time of year you visit, there is sure to be something to suit your interests and make your trip to Wallonia unforgettable.

CHAPTER 5 OUTSIDE THE CITIES

Welcome to the Ardennes region.

Welcome to the Ardennes region, a picturesque area in southeastern Belgium known for its rolling hills, dense forests, and winding rivers. The Ardennes covers an area of approximately 11,000 square kilometers and is home to a variety of small towns, villages, and natural attractions.

One of the main draws of the Ardennes is its stunning natural beauty.

The region is home to several nature reserves, including the Hautes Fagnes-Eifel Nature Park, which boasts over 4,000 hectares of wetlands, heathlands, and forests. Visitors can hike, bike, or horseback ride through the park, enjoying the breathtaking views along the way.

Another popular natural attraction in the Ardennes is the river Meuse, which winds its way through the region, offering opportunities for boating, fishing, and kayaking. Visitors can also explore the network of canals and waterways that connect the Meuse to other rivers and water bodies in the area.

The Ardennes is also rich in history and culture. The region played a significant role in both World War I and World War II, and visitors can explore several historic sites and monuments, including the Battle of the Bulge Memorial and the Bastogne War Museum. The region is also home to a number of medieval castles and fortresses, such as the Castle of Bouillon and the Castle of Modave.

In addition to its natural and historic attractions, the Ardennes is also known for its delicious cuisine. The region is famous for its hearty meat dishes, such as wild boar stew and roasted game, as well as its artisanal cheeses and locally produced beers. Visitors can also indulge in the region's sweet specialties, such as the famous Belgian waffles and Liège-style sugared bread.

Whether you're looking to explore the great outdoors, immerse yourself in history and culture, or simply relax and indulge in some delicious food and drink, the Ardennes region has something to offer everyone. So why not come and experience this beautiful and diverse region for yourself?

5 must see attraction of ardenes region.

1. Hiking and biking trails

The Ardennes region in Belgium is a stunning area of natural beauty that offers a range of hiking and biking trails for visitors to explore. With its rolling hills, dense forests, and winding rivers, the region is a paradise for outdoor enthusiasts.

Hiking Trails:

There are numerous hiking trails throughout the Ardennes, ranging from easy walks to more challenging hikes. The region is home to several national parks, including the Hautes Fagnes-Eifel Nature Park, which offers over 200 kilometers of hiking trails. Other popular hiking areas include the Ninglinspo Valley, the Hoge Kempen National Park, and the Lesse Valley. Visitors can choose from circular walks, multi-day treks, and guided tours.

One of the most popular hiking trails in the Ardennes is the GR 5, a long-distance trail that stretches from the North Sea to the Mediterranean. The trail passes through the Ardennes, offering hikers the chance to explore some of the region's most scenic areas. The GR 571, also known as the Transardennaise, is another popular long-distance trail that offers stunning views of the region.

Biking Trails:

The Ardennes is also a popular destination for biking enthusiasts, with a range of trails suitable for all levels of experience.

The region is home to several mountain bike trails, including the Vennbahn Trail, which stretches for 125 kilometers from Aachen to Troisvierges. Other popular mountain bike trails include the Eislek Trail and the Lesse Valley Trail.

For road cyclists, the Ardennes offers a range of scenic routes, including the famous La Redoute climb, which is part of the Liege-Bastogne-Liege race. The region also offers a number of cycle routes that take in the area's picturesque villages, rolling hills, and stunning landscapes.

Guided Tours:

For visitors who want to explore the Ardennes with the help of a guide, there are a number of companies that offer guided hiking and biking tours. These tours can be customized to suit individual needs and interests and are led by experienced guides who are familiar with the region.

Overall, the Ardennes region in Belgium is a must-visit destination for anyone who loves the great outdoors. With its stunning scenery, diverse hiking and biking trails, and range of guided tours, it is the perfect place to escape the hustle and bustle of city life and immerse yourself in nature.

2. Caves of Han

The Caves of Han is a popular tourist attraction located in the Ardennes region of Belgium. The cave system is made up of a series of underground chambers and passageways, filled with stunning natural formations, including stalactites, stalagmites, and underground rivers.

The Caves of Han are located within the Han-sur-Lesse Wildlife Park, which covers over 250 hectares of forests, meadows, and rocky outcrops. Visitors can explore the park on foot, by electric cart, or on a safari-style tour that takes them through the heart of the park, where they can see a variety of wild animals, including bison, deer, wolves, and lynx.

To enter the Caves of Han, visitors must take a guided tour, which lasts approximately 1 hour and 15 minutes. The tour begins with a descent into the underground chambers, where visitors are immediately struck by the sheer size and beauty of the caves.

The guides explain the geological processes that have formed the cave system over millions of years, and point out some of the most impressive formations, such as the stalactites that hang from the ceiling and the stalagmites that rise from the cave floor.

As visitors make their way through the caves, they can also admire the beautiful underground rivers and pools, which are home to a variety of subterranean species, including crayfish and blind salamanders. The guides also provide information about the history of the caves, including their use as a shelter by prehistoric humans.

At the end of the tour, visitors can take a ride on the "tramway des Grottes," a small train that takes them back to the surface. Along the way, they can enjoy stunning views of the surrounding park and learn more about the wildlife that calls it home.

Overall, the Caves of Han is a must-see attraction for anyone visiting Belgium. With its stunning natural beauty, rich history, and impressive array of wildlife, it offers a unique and unforgettable experience for visitors of all ages.

3. Euro Space Center

The Euro Space Center is a must-visit attraction for anyone interested in space exploration and science. Located in Transinne, Belgium, the center offers visitors an immersive and educational experience that takes them on a journey through the history of space exploration and the wonders of the universe.

The Euro Space Center is divided into several different areas, each offering its own unique experiences and attractions. Visitors start their journey in the entrance hall, where they can learn about the different planets in our solar system and see a scale model of the International Space Station.

Next, visitors move on to the Discovery Hall, where they can explore a variety of interactive exhibits and simulations. Here, visitors can experience the feeling of walking on the moon, learn about the mechanics of space travel, and even try their hand at piloting a space shuttle.

One of the most exciting areas of the Euro Space Center is the Astronaut Hall, where visitors can learn about the experiences of real-life astronauts and what it takes to become one. The hall features a number of exhibits, including a mock-up of a space shuttle cockpit and a replica of the Russian Mir space station.

In addition to the exhibits and simulations, the Euro Space Center also offers a number of educational programs and workshops. These programs are designed to give visitors a deeper understanding of space exploration and the scientific principles behind it.

For those interested in more hands-on experiences, the Euro Space Center also offers a range of outdoor activities. Visitors can take part in a variety of team-building exercises, such as building a rocket or participating in a space mission simulation.

Overall, the Euro Space Center is an exciting and educational attraction that offers something for visitors of all ages. With its interactive exhibits, immersive simulations, and educational programs, it is the perfect destination for anyone interested in space exploration and the wonders of the universe.

4. **Bastogne War Museum**

5.

The Bastogne War Museum is a must-visit attraction for anyone interested in World War II history. Located in the town of Bastogne, Belgium, the museum offers visitors a comprehensive and immersive experience that takes them back in time to the events that unfolded during the Battle of the Bulge.

The Battle of the Bulge was a significant military engagement that took place during the winter of 1944-1945.

The German army launched a surprise offensive against Allied forces, with the intention of splitting their lines and capturing the port of Antwerp. The battle was fought in the densely forested Ardennes region of Belgium, and it lasted for six weeks, resulting in heavy casualties on both sides.

The Bastogne War Museum provides visitors with an in-depth look at the events leading up to the battle, the strategies employed by both sides, and the experiences of soldiers and civilians who lived through it. The museum is housed in a modern building that blends seamlessly with the surrounding landscape.

Upon entering the museum, visitors are greeted with a large-scale projection of a battle scene, setting the tone for the rest of the exhibit. The museum is divided into different sections, each of which offers a unique perspective on the battle. Interactive displays, multimedia exhibits, and personal accounts from soldiers and civilians help to bring the history of the battle to life.

One of the most moving exhibits in the museum is the Hall of Faces. This exhibit displays the photographs and names of over 76,000 soldiers who fought in the Battle of the Bulge, paying tribute to their sacrifice and bravery.

Visitors can also explore a replica of a battlefield, complete with authentic tanks and military equipment. The exhibit provides a glimpse into the harsh conditions that soldiers faced during the battle and offers a unique perspective on the tactics employed by both sides.

The Bastogne War Museum also offers guided tours and educational programs for schools and groups. The museum is accessible for visitors with disabilities and has a gift shop where visitors can purchase books, souvenirs, and memorabilia related to the battle.

Overall, the Bastogne War Museum is a moving tribute to the soldiers who fought in the Battle of the Bulge and a reminder of the importance of remembering and learning from the past. A visit to the museum is an essential part of any trip to Belgium for anyone interested in history, military strategy, or World War II.

6. Durbuy Christmas Markets

Durbuy, a charming medieval town located in the Ardennes region of Belgium, is a popular destination for visitors year-round. However, during the Christmas season, the town transforms into a magical winter wonderland, with the Durbuy Christmas Markets taking center stage.

The Durbuy Christmas Markets are held every year from late November to early January, with the town's picturesque streets and squares decorated with thousands of twinkling lights and festive decorations. The markets offer a wide range of stalls selling everything from handmade crafts and gifts to traditional Belgian foods and drinks.

One of the highlights of the Durbuy Christmas Markets is the ice-skating rink, which is set up in the town's central square. Visitors can rent skates and glide around the rink while surrounded by the festive atmosphere of the markets. There are also a number of carnival rides and attractions for children, making it a great destination for families.

In addition to the markets, visitors can also take part in a few other holiday-themed activities in Durbuy. The town's Christmas tree is a sight to behold, towering over the town square and adorned with sparkling lights and ornaments. There are also a number of concerts and performances held throughout the season, featuring local musicians and dancers.

One of the highlights of the Durbuy Christmas Markets is the food and drink on offer. Visitors can indulge in traditional Belgian delicacies such as waffles, speculoos biscuits, and hot chocolate, as well as hearty stews and soups to warm up on cold winter days. There are also a number of stalls selling mulled wine, Belgian beer, and other festive drinks. Overall, the Durbuy Christmas Markets offer a truly magical experience for visitors of all ages. From the festive decorations and lights to the delicious food and drink, it's a destination that captures the holiday spirit in a unique and special way. If you're planning a trip to Belgium during the Christmas season, be sure to add the Durbuy Christmas Markets to your itinerary.

Welcome to Coastal region.

Welcome to the Coastal Region of Belgium, a beautiful stretch of coastline that spans nearly 67 kilometers along the North Sea. This region is home to some of the country's most popular seaside resorts, picturesque fishing villages, and stunning beaches. The Coastal Region is in the Flemish province of West Flanders, and it is an ideal destination for beach lovers, nature enthusiasts, and anyone looking to escape the hustle and bustle of city life. Visitors can enjoy long walks along the beach, soak up the sun on a lounger, or take a refreshing dip in the sea.

One of the most popular destinations in the Coastal Region is the city of Ostend, a lively and cosmopolitan city that has been a favorite seaside resort for over a century. Visitors can stroll along the beach promenade, enjoy fresh seafood at one of the many restaurants, or visit the iconic Mercator ship museum.

Another must-see attraction in the Coastal Region is the town of Blankenberge, which boasts a long and wide sandy beach, a charming marina, and a bustling boardwalk. The town is also home to the Sea Life Marine Park, where visitors can get up close and personal with a variety of marine creatures.

For those looking for a more tranquil and secluded beach experience, the town of De Haan is a great option. This picturesque town features a long beach surrounded by sand dunes, as well as a beautiful park and several charming cafes and restaurants.

The Coastal Region is also known for its natural beauty, with several nature reserves and parks located along the coast.

The Zwin Nature Reserve is a must-visit for birdwatchers, with over 300 species of birds that can be observed throughout the year. The nature reserve also features a visitors' center, hiking trails, and a playground for children.

Overall, the Coastal Region of Belgium is a beautiful and diverse destination that offers something for everyone. Whether you're looking to soak up the sun on a sandy beach, explore charming seaside towns, or connect with nature, this region is sure to delight and inspire. So come and experience the magic of the Belgian coast for yourself!

5 must see attractions in the coastal region.

1. Ostend beaches

Ostend is a coastal city in Belgium, located in the Flemish region. It is known for its long stretches of sandy beaches and lively promenade, making it a popular destination for both locals and tourists. Here is a comprehensive guide to Ostend beaches:

Overview: Ostend beaches offer a great opportunity for visitors to enjoy the sun, sand, and sea. The beaches are located along the North Sea coast, and they stretch for miles, making it easy to find a spot to relax and soak up the sun. The beaches are well-maintained, and the water is clean and safe for swimming.

Beaches: The main beaches in Ostend are the Groot Strand and Klein Strand. Groot Strand is the largest beach in Ostend, and it is situated right in the heart of the city. The beach is very wide and has a lot of space for sunbathing, playing games, and other activities. Klein Strand is a smaller beach located to the east of Groot Strand, and it is more secluded and less crowded than the main beach.

Activities: There are plenty of activities to do at Ostend beaches. Visitors can swim, sunbathe, play beach volleyball or soccer, or rent a beach chair and umbrella. There are also a variety of water sports available, including surfing, windsurfing, and kiteboarding. Visitors can also take a stroll or bike ride along the promenade and enjoy the beautiful views of the sea.

Facilities: Ostend beaches have excellent facilities, including showers, changing rooms, and toilets. There are also a variety of beachside cafes and restaurants where visitors can grab a bite to eat or a refreshing drink. Beachgoers can rent chairs and umbrellas, and there are also plenty of options for renting water sports equipment.

Events: Ostend beaches host a variety of events throughout the year, including concerts, beach volleyball tournaments, and kite festivals. The city also has an annual sand sculpture festival, where artists from around the world create elaborate sculptures out of sand.

Accessibility: Ostend beaches are easily accessible by public transportation, with several bus and train options available. There are also plenty of parking options for those traveling by car. The beaches are also accessible to people with disabilities, with wheelchair ramps and accessible toilets available.

In conclusion, Ostend beaches are a great destination for anyone looking to enjoy the sun, sand, and sea. With their long stretches of sandy beaches, excellent facilities, and variety of activities, Ostend beaches are a must-visit destination for any traveler to Belgium.

2. Blankenberge pier

Blankenberge pier, located in the coastal town of Blankenberge, Belgium, is a popular attraction for both locals and tourists alike.

Originally built in 1933, the pier has undergone several renovations and additions over the years, making it a must-visit destination for anyone traveling to the Belgian coast.

The pier extends over 350 meters into the North Sea, offering stunning views of the coastline and the surrounding area. At the end of the pier, visitors will find a large observation tower that provides a panoramic view of the sea and the town of Blankenberge.

In addition to the observation tower, the pier also features a number of other attractions and amenities. Visitors can enjoy a variety of food and drink options at the pier's many cafes and restaurants, including fresh seafood, Belgian waffles, and ice cream.

For those looking for a bit of adventure, there are several activities available at the pier. Visitors can take a ride on the pier's Ferris wheel, which offers breathtaking views of the North Sea and the surrounding area. There is also a small amusement park with rides for both children and adults.

Fishing is also a popular activity on the pier, with many visitors casting their lines into the sea in hopes of catching a variety of fish, including cod, plaice, and sole. Fishing equipment can be rented from several vendors located on the pier.

Throughout the year, Blankenberge pier hosts a variety of events and activities, including concerts, festivals, and fireworks displays. The pier is also a popular spot for watching the sunset, with visitors often gathering at the end of the pier to watch as the sun sinks below the horizon.

Overall, Blankenberge pier is a must-visit destination for anyone traveling to the Belgian coast. With its stunning views, delicious food and drink options, and variety of activities and events, the pier offers something for everyone. Whether you're looking for a bit of adventure or simply want to relax and take in the beauty of the North Sea, Blankenberge pier is a destination that should not be missed.

3. Zwin Nature Park

Zwin Nature Park is a stunning natural reserve located in the coastal town of Knokke-Heist, in the province of West Flanders. The park covers an area of approximately 158 hectares and is home to a wide variety of plant and animal species, including many rare and endangered ones.

The park is situated along the coast and features a diverse landscape of dunes, mudflats, salt marshes, and tidal creeks. This unique combination of habitats provides a home to many different types of birds, including some of the rarest species in Europe. Visitors can witness migratory birds such as the European spoonbill, black-tailed godwit, and avocet as they make their way through the park.

Zwin Nature Park offers a number of different activities for visitors to enjoy. The park has a network of walking and cycling paths that allow visitors to explore the different habitats and observe the birds and other wildlife. There are also guided tours available, led by knowledgeable experts who can provide more in-depth information about the park's ecology and history.

One of the highlights of the park is the birdwatching tower, which offers panoramic views of the reserve and its inhabitants. From the tower, visitors can observe a variety of different bird species, including storks, ospreys, and peregrine falcons.

In addition to its natural beauty, Zwin Nature Park also features a number of facilities for visitors, including a visitor center, a gift shop, and a café. The visitor center offers interactive exhibits and displays that educate visitors about the park's ecology and the importance of conservation efforts.

Zwin Nature Park is also dedicated to sustainability and conservation efforts, with a focus on protecting and preserving the unique habitats and species that call the park home. The park has a number of initiatives in place to reduce its environmental impact, such as using renewable energy sources and promoting sustainable tourism practices.

Overall, Zwin Nature Park is a must-visit destination for nature lovers and birdwatchers. With its stunning landscapes, diverse wildlife, and dedication to conservation, it is a true gem of the Belgian coast.

3. Sea Life Blankenberge

Sea Life Blankenberge is a must-visit attraction for anyone interested in marine life and ocean conservation. Located in the seaside town of Blankenberge, Belgium, Sea Life Blankenberge is a world-renowned aquarium that offers visitors an up-close and personal look at some of the most fascinating creatures that call the ocean home.

The aquarium is home to over 50 different displays, with more than 2,500 animals from 146 species. Visitors can marvel at the colorful fish, sea turtles, and rays, and learn about the diverse ecosystems that exist within our oceans. The aquarium also has several interactive exhibits that allow visitors to touch and interact with some of the animals, including starfish and sea urchins.

One of the highlights of Sea Life Blankenberge is the ocean tunnel, a 70-meter-long walkway that takes visitors through a stunning underwater world. As you walk through the tunnel, you'll be surrounded by schools of fish, sharks, and even a giant sea turtle.

The aquarium also has a strong focus on conservation, with a number of initiatives designed to raise awareness about the threats facing our oceans and the animals that live within them. Visitors can learn about Sea Life's efforts to protect endangered species, reduce plastic pollution, and promote sustainable fishing practices.

In addition to the exhibits, Sea Life Blankenberge also offers a range of educational programs for children and adults. These programs cover a variety of topics, from marine biology and conservation to the history of the aquarium and its animals. Visitors can also attend feeding sessions and talks by the aquarium's expert staff, who are passionate about sharing their knowledge and love of the ocean with others.

Sea Life Blankenberge is open year-round, making it a great destination for visitors to Belgium at any time of the year. It is easily accessible by public transportation, and there are several nearby hotels and restaurants for those looking to make a day of their visit.

Overall, Sea Life Blankenberge is a must-visit attraction for anyone interested in marine life, conservation, and the wonders of the ocean. With its stunning displays, interactive exhibits, and educational programs, it is a destination that will leave a lasting impression on visitors of all ages.

4. Oostende Kitesurfing Festival

The Oostende Kitesurfing Festival is an annual event that takes place in the coastal city of Ostend, Belgium. It is one of the most exciting and popular kitesurfing events in the country, attracting kitesurfers from all over Europe.

The festival is typically held in late summer and takes place over several days. It features a wide range of activities and events for kitesurfers of all skill levels, including competitions, exhibitions, and workshops. Visitors can watch some of the world's best kitesurfers in action as they perform stunning aerial tricks and maneuvers in the waves.

One of the highlights of the festival is the kiteboarding competition, which features both amateur and professional athletes competing in a variety of categories. The competition is open to both men and women, and the winners are awarded prizes and recognition for their achievements.

In addition to the competition, the festival also features several workshops and seminars for kitesurfers of all skill levels. Visitors can learn about the latest techniques, equipment, and safety practices from experts in the field.

Beyond the kitesurfing activities, the festival also offers a range of entertainment options for visitors. There are live music performances, food and drink stalls, and a lively atmosphere that attracts visitors from all over Belgium and beyond.

Ostend itself is a charming coastal city with a rich cultural heritage and a long history as a popular seaside resort. Visitors can explore the city's sandy beaches, historic architecture, and numerous restaurants and shops. The city is also home to a number of museums and cultural attractions, including the James Ensor House, which is dedicated to the works of the famous Belgian painter. Overall, the Oostende Kitesurfing Festival is an exciting event that offers a unique blend of sport, entertainment, and culture. Whether you're a kitesurfing enthusiast or just looking for a fun and unique way to experience Belgium's stunning coastal region, this festival is not to be missed.

Accommodations outside the city

Belgium has many charming towns and villages outside of its major cities, and visitors can find a range of accommodations to suit their needs. Whether you're looking for a cozy bed and breakfast or a luxurious spa hotel, you'll find plenty of options outside of the city.

Bed and Breakfasts:

One popular option for travelers looking for accommodation outside of the city is bed and breakfast. Belgium has many charming B&Bs located in picturesque countryside settings, offering a chance to experience the country's natural beauty up close. Many of these properties offer homemade breakfasts using local ingredients, and some may also offer additional services such as bike rentals or guided tours.

Guesthouses:

Another popular accommodation option in Belgium is guesthouses. Like B&Bs, guesthouses offer a more personal and intimate experience than larger hotels. Many guesthouses are in historic buildings, such as converted farmhouses or manor houses, and offer unique architectural features and charming decor. Some guesthouses may also offer meals, as well as activities such as hiking or horseback riding.

Hotels:

For those seeking more traditional hotel accommodations, there are also plenty of options outside of the city. Many hotels in rural areas offer stunning views of the surrounding landscape and are often located near popular tourist attractions. Some hotels may offer additional amenities such as spas, pools, and restaurants.

Camping:

For those who enjoy outdoor adventures, camping is a popular option in Belgium. There are many campsites located throughout the country, ranging from basic sites for tents to fully-equipped campgrounds with RV hookups and facilities. Camping is a great way to experience Belgium's natural beauty up close and is often a more affordable option than traditional accommodations.

Overall, visitors to Belgium have a wide range of accommodations to choose from outside of the city. From cozy bed and breakfasts to luxurious spa hotels, there is something for everyone. When planning your trip, consider the location and activities you'll be doing to find the perfect accommodation to fit your needs.

Food and drink

While Belgium is known for its excellent cuisine and beer culture, visitors can also find plenty of delicious food and drink outside of the cities. From cozy countryside restaurants to picturesque vineyards, there is something for every food and wine lover in Belgium.

Flemish Stews and Seafood in the Coastal Towns

Belgium's North Sea coast is dotted with picturesque towns and villages that are famous for their seafood and traditional Flemish stews. In towns like Oostende and De Haan, visitors can enjoy freshly caught shrimp, mussels, and fish prepared in a variety of ways, from classic moules-frites to grilled fish served with local vegetables.

For those looking for heartier fare, Flemish stews like waterzooi and carbonnade are popular dishes in the coastal region. These stews feature tender pieces of meat, such as beef or chicken, cooked with a variety of vegetables in a rich broth flavored with beer or wine.

Wine Tasting in the Ardennes

The Ardennes region of Belgium is known for its rolling hills, dense forests, and winding rivers, as well as its excellent wine. The region is home to several vineyards and wineries that produce a range of red, white, and sparkling wines.

Visitors can take a wine tasting tour of the region, visiting small family-run wineries as well as larger operations. The wines of the Ardennes are known for their complex flavors and aromas, with varieties ranging from pinot noir and chardonnay to riesling and pinot gris.

Trappist Beer and Cheese in Chimay

The town of Chimay, located in the southern region of Wallonia, is home to one of Belgium's most famous trappist breweries. The Chimay Brewery produces a range of beers, including the popular Chimay Blue, Red, and White varieties, which are brewed using traditional methods by the monks of the Scourmont Abbey.

In addition to its beer, Chimay is also known for its cheese, which is made by the same monks using milk from the abbey's own cows. Visitors can take a tour of the brewery and cheese factory, as well as sample the products in the on-site restaurant.

Chocolate and Waffles in the Belgian Countryside

Belgium is famous for its chocolate and waffles, and visitors can find delicious examples of both in the country's rural areas. In towns like Bruges and Leuven, visitors can visit artisanal chocolate shops and watch chocolatiers at work, creating exquisite pralines and truffles.

Belgium's famous waffles are also a treat to enjoy in the countryside, with small roadside stands and cafes serving up sweet and savory varieties. Toppings like fresh fruit, whipped cream, and Nutella are popular choices for sweet waffles, while savory versions may be topped with cheese, bacon, or ham.

In conclusion, visitors to Belgium who venture outside the cities can find a wealth of delicious food and drink options to explore. Whether it's enjoying seafood on the coast, tasting wine in the Ardennes, or savoring trappist beer and cheese in Chimay, there is something to please every palate.

Belgium deliciuos cuisines

Conclusion

In conclusion, Belgium is a fascinating and unique country with a rich history and culture that is well worth exploring. From the historic cities of Brussels, Bruges, and Ghent, to the beautiful countryside of the Ardennes and Flanders, there is something for everyone in this small but vibrant country.

Visitors to Belgium can indulge in world-famous Belgian chocolate and beer, wander through medieval streets, marvel at the stunning architecture of art nouveau buildings, and explore some of the most impressive art collections in Europe. The country is also home to a thriving fashion and design scene, making it a must-visit destination for style-conscious travelers.

Belgium is a destination that can be enjoyed all year round, with each season bringing its own unique attractions. Springtime brings the stunning display of colorful tulips in the Keukenhof Gardens, while summer sees a plethora of festivals and events throughout the country. Fall is the ideal time to explore the natural beauty of the Ardennes, while winter brings the magic of the Christmas markets and festive cheer.

Travelers to Belgium can expect a warm and friendly welcome from locals, and a well-developed tourism infrastructure with excellent transport links and a wide range of accommodation options. Whether you're a solo traveler, a couple looking for a romantic getaway, or a family in search of adventure, Belgium has something to offer.

In summary, a trip to Belgium promises a unique and unforgettable experience, filled with history, culture, food, and drink. So, pack your bags, prepare your itinerary, and get ready to explore this fascinating and enchanting country.

Printed in Great Britain
by Amazon